Nature's
Wonderlands
National Parks of the World

Nature's Wonderlands

National Parks of the World

National
Geographic
Society

Nature's Wonderlands
National Parks of the World

Published by
The National Geographic
Society

Gilbert M. Grosvenor
*President and
Chairman of the Board*

Owen R. Anderson
Executive Vice President

Robert L. Breeden
*Senior Vice President,
Publications and
Educational Media*

Prepared by
National Geographic
Book Service

Charles O. Hyman
Director

Ross S. Bennett
Associate Director

Margaret Sedeen
Managing Editor

Susan C. Eckert
Director of Research

Staff for this book

Robert M. Poole
Editor

Leah Bendavid-Val
Illustrations Editor

David M. Seager
Art Director

Jean Kaplan Teichroew
Assistant Editor

Jennifer Gorham Ackerman
Mary B. Dickinson
Carol Bittig Lutyk
Jonathan B. Tourtellot
Lynn Addison Yorke
Editor-Writers

Gretchen C. Bordelon
Paulette L. Claus
Marguerite Suarez Dunn
Anne E. Ely
Joyce B. Marshall
Kimberly I. Steere
Penelope A. Timbers
Editorial Researchers

Anne E. Ely
Map Coordinator

Mark V. Smith
Geography Intern

Lise Swinson Sajewski
Style

Charlotte Golin
Design Assistant

David Ross
Illustrations Researcher

Michael S. Frost
Illustrations Assistant

Karen F. Edwards
Traffic Manager

R. Gary Colbert
*Senior Administrative
Assistant*

Teresita Cóquia Sison
Editorial Assistant

Diane L. Coleman
Indexer

Richard S. Wain
Production Manager

Andrea Crosman
*Assistant Production
Manager*

Emily F. Gwynn
Production Assistant

*Manufacturing and
Quality Management*

John T. Dunn
Director

David V. Evans
Manager

Ratri Banerjee
Jennifer Davidson
Caroline Sheen
Anne E. Withers
Contributors

Previous pages: Sunrise at
Grand Teton National Park, Wyoming
By Ron Thomas

First edition: 110,000 copies
304 pages, 233 illustrations,
22 maps.

Contents

A World of Parks

A nation's parks should be sacred places, where time stands still and silence rules, where crime, war, pollution, and heedless development do not intrude.

But national parks exist in the real world, and all too often the reminders of that reality break through the borders: the traffic that makes it risky to follow Wordsworth's footsteps across the Lake District National Park of England; the poachers who slaughter endangered rhinos in Kenya's Meru National Park; the canals and farms that threaten to dry up Everglades National Park; the graziers who destroy tiger habitat in India's Ranthambhore National Park. No matter how big or how isolated, each park is vulnerable in some way.

Despite that, the world's parks do enrich us all, by saving precious resources. Garajonay National Park protects scarce water supplies in Spain's Canary Islands. Tikal National Park in Guatemala preserves Maya temples, reminders of a once great empire. Other parks hold whole ecosystems in safekeeping for the future: Manú Biosphere Reserve, a Peruvian rain forest park almost the size of New Jersey, contains an awesome diversity of plants and animals, many of them yet unknown to science. Parks also serve as living laboratories for scientific study, as in the Soviet Union's Astrakhan' State Nature Reserve, and the Great Barrier Reef Marine Park of Australia.

Parks rejuvenate the human spirit as well. They provide the occasional island of calm in a clamorous world. Jasper National Park of Canada is such a sanctuary, where you can spend an afternoon doing nothing more complicated than watching the snow fall on silent mountains.

Places like that, increasingly rare, are the places we celebrate in this book. If there were space for it, we would celebrate all of the world's parks and wilderness areas. Though often battered and imperfect, they are all we have, and they are beyond value.
Gilbert M. Grosvenor

The world has more than 4,000 national parks and protected areas. This map locates but a few, which are featured in this book. They illustrate some of the roles a nation's parks play—to preserve areas of scenic and cultural worth, to provide places for study, recreation, and wildlife, to set aside ecosystems for the future.

Ocean

Pallas-Ounastunturi N.P.

Sarek N.P.

Thingvellir N.P.

Lake District N.P.

Prioksko-Terrasnyy
State Nature Reserve

ASIA

North
Pacific
Ocean

EUROPE

Astrakan'
State Nature Reserve

Bayerischer Wald N.P.

Gran Paradiso N.P.

La Vanoise N.P.

Kavkaz State Nature Reserve

Abruzzo N.P.

Fuji-Hakone-Izu N.P.

Doñana N.P.

Jiuzhaigou N.P.

Ashizuri-Uwakai N.P.

Wolong Natural Reserve

Sobo-Katamuki N.P.

Tassili-n-Ajjer N.P.

Sagarmatha N.P.

Ranthambhore N.P.

Taal Volcano Island N.P.

AFRICA

Virunga N.P.

Masai Mara
National Reserve

Serengeti N.P.

Kilimanjaro N.P.

Ngorongoro
Conservation
Area

Indian Ocean

OCEANIA

Bromo-Tengger-
Semeru N.P.

Kakadu N.P.

Great Barrier Reef
Marine Park

Chobe N.P.
Moremi
Wildlife
Reserve

AUSTRALIA

Namib-Naukluft Park

Uluru (Ayers Rock-
Mount Olga) N.P.

South
Atlantic
Ocean

Nambung N.P.

Egmont N.P.

Cradle Mountain-
Lake St. Clair N.P.

Mount Cook N.P.

Fiordland N.P.

North America

The national parks were born in North America, bot
the dream and the realization—Yellowstone in 1872
Banff in 1885, Glacier and Yoho in 1886, Bosque El
Chico in 1898. North America has never relinquishe
its lead. More land is devoted to national parks and
protected areas in the northern half of the New Wor
than on any other continent.

Most of North America falls into the biogeographi
realm called the Nearctic. Of the 22 biogeographic
provinces within that realm, 20 are represented in n
tional parks and protected areas. There are more tha
300 parks in the Nearctic, and more than 540,000
square miles of protected land—an area nearly the
size of Alaska.

Greenland National Park, established by Denmark
in 1974, is, at 270,000 square miles, the largest national park on earth. Redwood National Park protect
the tallest living thing, the coast redwood *Sequoia
sempervirens* (upwards of 350 feet tall). Yosemite N
tional Park preserves the most massive—the big tree
Sequoiadendron giganteum (upwards of 35 feet in d
ameter). Mammoth Cave National Park covers the
longest known cave system on—or under—earth
(more than 300 miles long, on five connecting levels
Denali National Park is home to the continent's larg
est herbivore, the moose, as well as North America's
highest point, the 20,320-foot summit of Mount Mc-
Kinley. Gates of the Arctic National Park in Alaska
preserves part of the range of the caribou, in the
greatest ungulate herds surviving outside the Serengeti. Wood Buffalo National Park, at the border of Alberta and the Northwest Territories, provides a have
for what was once the greatest herd of all, the bison.
Grasslands National Park, proclaimed in 1981 in Sas
katchewan, protects a vestige of those once endless
prairies that moved painter and adventurer George
Catlin to propose a *"nation's Park"* in 1832.

One of our luxuries in North America is to criticize
our parks. Yosemite is too crowded, it is often said.

United States

Big Bend National Park

A rare winter snowfall lingers in
Big Bend National Park, which
takes its name from a horse-
shoe turn in the Rio Grande on
the southwestern border of
Texas. Except for the river
along the park's southern edge
and the Chisos Mountains that
rise nearly 8,000 feet like temperate islands at the park's
center, Big Bend is desert. The
muted shades of winter will
give way to a burst of color in
the spring after dormant wild-
flower seeds are washed by a
rainfall or two. Most of the
park's 60 or so cactus species
also bloom in the spring but
spend the rest of the year
like these prickly pears—
unadorned and storing precious water in their fleshy,
waxy-coated stems.

here is smog and crime in the valley; we are loving
 the place to death. Many of us who like our wilderness straight believe that parks are best managed by
god and nature. The 1988 Yellowstone conflagration
demonstrated this. So did the park service decision,
 the early 1970s, to abandon decades of erosion con-
ol at Cape Hatteras National Seashore, where the
overnment had spent millions to keep barrier islands
om moving, as such islands are inclined to do.

 But, for perspective, it is good to travel with some-
ne from one of the more trammeled continents,
omeone without that luxury to criticize. One recent
utumn, in Riding Mountain National Park of Mani-
ba, a Chinese biologist named Quan Dong ap-
roached a trapped coyote. The coyote, a nearly
rown pup, was calm in the trap. Quan Dong, for his
art was very excited.

 There are few wild animals left in China. No coun-
y has been longer used, or more altered, by techno-
gical man. Once 70 percent of temperate China was
rested, now only 8 percent. Quan had studied pan-
as, but only from a distance. Never had he been so
ose to a wild animal.

 After Quan's mentor and colleague, biologist Paul
aquet, immobilized and muzzled the coyote, Quan
nelt beside it. He could not keep his hands off the
up, and they wandered all over it, as if desperately
ying to *absorb* the animal. Quan's gentle mauling of
e coyote was poignant—the biologist starved for bi-
logy—but Paquet was uneasy. He wanted to limit the
andling time, to weigh the coyote quickly, fit it with
 radio collar, and send it on its way.

 "   uan," he said. "That's not how we do it."
 Quan did not seem to hear. He felt the legs, stroked
e coyote's hackles. "No, Quan!" Paquet repeated,
ut Quan, in a trance, kept running his fingers along
e coyote's mouth, feeling the teeth. *"No, Quan!"* Pa-
uet yelled. Finally Quan heard and desisted.

 The parks of North America, Quan Dong's eager
ands testified, are an embarrassment of riches.

United States

**Great Smoky Mountains
National Park**

A perfect canvas for autumn's
artistry, Great Smoky woodlands spread over 800 square
miles of upland terrain along
the border between Tennes-
see and North Carolina. Here,
in the most extensive virgin forests in the eastern United
States, reside 130 tree species—as many as in all of Europe. Tangles of blooming
plants called heath balds—
twisted masses of rhododen-
dron, laurel, sand myrtle, and
azalea—grow here and no-
where else in the world. A classic example of evolution in
isolation, 26 species of sala-
manders live in the park, their
habitats sometimes separated
by no more than a few miles of
lowland where conditions are
unfavorable for their survival.
Some are aquatic, some terrestrial. Some climb trees at
night; others never leave the
forest floor.

Everglades National Park

"Here are no lofty peaks seeking the sky, no mighty glaciers or rushing streams," said President Harry S. Truman at the 1947 dedication of Everglades National Park. "Here is land, tranquil in its quiet beauty, serving not as the source of water but as the last receiver of it." For more than 5,000 years this subtropical wilderness of saw grass, tree islands, and mangrove forests was the last receiver of annual freshwater overflow from Lake Okeechobee, 90 miles north of the park. Water from the lake spread southward in a river just inches deep and up to 50 miles wide. But along with the development of south Florida's coastal megalopolis came a system of canals and levees redirecting water to aid agriculture and ease the threat of flooding. Now survival of the park's fragile and complex ecosystem, including such creatures as the great egret and more than 300 other bird species, depends entirely on human management of water, the lifeblood of the Everglades.

Tom Algire

United States

Redwood National Park

"These great trees belong to the silences and milleniums. They seem, indeed, to be forms of immortality, standing there among the transitory shapes of time."

They rise, the coast redwoods thus described by poet Edwin Markham, from a temperate belt of summer fog and winter rain stretching along the Pacific Ocean from southwestern Oregon to central California. Some of them are more than ten centuries old. Protected by national park status since 1968, these redwoods and their relatives, the giant sequoias found only on the western slope of California's Sierra Nevada, are descendants of sequoias that covered much of the Northern Hemisphere before the last ice age.

United States

Yosemite National Park

The sheer face of El Capitan— the largest exposed granite monolith in the world—towers 3,000 feet above snow-clad Yosemite Valley in California. The park's winter snows, though heavy, are a mere dusting compared to the crush of glacial ice that began to sculpture Yosemite's distinctive granite features more than a million years ago. A river of ice filled Yosemite Valley from rim to rim and carved pillars, cliffs, and spires. Ice in tributary valleys shaped leaping-off points for some of the highest waterfalls in the world. In the High Sierra, glaciers unbounded by valley walls spread in broad sheets over mountain peaks. Melting left glacial lakes; some eventually filled with silt to become sloping mountain meadows carpeted with wildflowers in the spring.

United States

Grand Canyon National Park

It is "grandiose . . . sublime . . . illusory," wrote American author Henry Miller. It is like "twenty Matterhorns blazing with alpine glow," wrote British diplomat Harold Nicolson. "Maybe the Grand Canyon . . . was God's main purpose," wrote author Alistair Cooke.

The Arizona landmark is one mile deep. It chronicles almost two billion years of earth's history, inscribed in layer upon layer of sediment on canyon walls: a record of inland seas and deserts and the creatures that inhabited them. It began some 65 million years ago with the uplifting of the Colorado Plateau and subsequent carving by the Colorado River. Its creation continues today as weather erodes the canyon walls and the Colorado, thickened during flash floods with silt, sand, and rock, cuts like liquid sandpaper into the canyon floor. "I thought I could imagine a better Grand Canyon did I?" wrote British author J. B. Priestley. "Well, cried Reality, take a look at this!"

17

Michael D. Yandell

Yellowstone River plunges 308 feet through the rugged canyon of the Lower Falls. Yellow sandstone bluffs near the mouth of the Yellowstone gave the river—and the nation's first national park—its name.

An Idea Unfolds

The National Park System has been called the best idea America ever had. Idealistic. Democratic. Visionary. Also, a bundle of contradictions, a prickly mix of opposing values, challenges and frustrations, ironies and compromises. Yellowstone is the oldest national park in the system; Great Basin the newest. In the century or so between their foundings, 47 United States national parks have come into being. And yet, just what these parks should be and do is still a subject of heated debate.

The conflict over the national park idea is rooted in the philosophical revolutions Americans have been through in the last three centuries, trying to make up their minds how they feel about nature. Colonial governor William Bradford summed up a lot of fashionable thinking in 1620 when he described America's virgin land as "hideous and desolate . . . full of wild beasts and wild men." To colonists the howling wilderness of the New World was an adversary, a dangerous place to be conquered and subdued.

Their descendants made short work of the task. By the mid-19th century, settlers and lumbermen had civilized and exploited much of the East. As more and more land fell to ax and plow, some Americans began to see wilderness in a new light—and mourned its loss. America's wild land was unique, they said, a source of national pride and cultural identity. It had shaped the character of its countrymen. "A fig for your Italian scenery!" cried one patriot. "This is the land . . . to feel your soul expand under the mighty influences of nature! . . ." Wild country was also an antidote to urban crowding, drudgery, and materialism. "Our lives," said Henry David Thoreau, "need the relief of [the wilderness] where the pine flourishes and the jay still screams."

In 1832 artist George Catlin suggested making a large area of the Great Plains into a "*nation's Park,* containing man and beast, in all the wild freshness of their nature's beauty." For pioneers, the idea of pre-

19

Yellowstone National Park

3,472 Square Miles

Largest national park in the contiguous United States, Yellowstone lies on a broad volcanic plateau along the ridge of the Rocky Mountains. There are 370 miles of paved roads at Yellowstone and 1,000 miles of trails winding through forested mountains and open meadows. There is a canyon with a waterfall almost twice Niagara's height, a mountain of volcanic glass, a fossil forest 50 million years old, and a deep blue pearl of a lake. There are grizzly bears, bison, bald eagles, and trumpeter swans. But the park's most popular attraction is its 10,000 thermal features—steaming geysers and fumaroles, boiling hot springs and bubbling mud pots—vivid reminders of the volcanic forces that shape the region. Probably the best known of the United States national parks, Yellowstone attracts more than two million visitors each year.

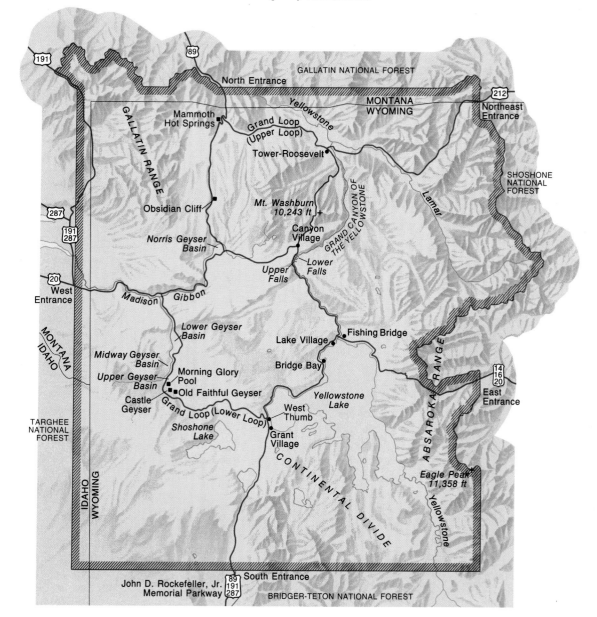

Old Faithful shoots straight up 100 feet and more, bursting into a roiling cloud of steam and spray. On average, the famous geyser erupts every 78 minutes.

NEXT PAGES: Mineral deposits build giant, encrusted basins at Minerva Terrace in Mammoth Hot Springs.

Jeremy Schmidt

serving land in an untamed state seemed absurd, but for a growing number of city dwellers, it fired the imagination.

The U. S. government first moved to protect a natural landscape in 1864, granting Yosemite Valley and a grove of giant Sierra redwoods to the state of California. Eight years later, a more sweeping proposal found its way to the desk of President Ulysses S. Grant. On March 1, 1872, Grant signed a bill establishing roughly 3,400 square miles of Montana and northwestern Wyoming—a land of spouting geysers, boiling mud pools, and jagged peaks—as Yellowstone National Park, to be "set apart as a public park or pleasureing ground for the benefit and enjoyment of the people." The nation's—and the world's—first national park was born.

The founding legislation for this public preserve provided no practical guidance and no firm definition of the national park idea. Rather, it launched a stimulating experiment in the stewardship of wild land, an experiment since repeated by more than a hundred countries around the world.

The last thing Yellowstone's founders wanted was a true wilderness. More like a giant national playground, a "colossal sort of junketing-place," as *Scribner's Monthly* called it. These pioneer preservationists were struck by the "remarkable curiosities" and "beautiful decorations" of Yellowstone—geysers, hot springs, canyons, falls—and wanted to protect them from private or commercial exploitation. The new national park was to belong to the public.

In Yellowstone's early years, public enjoyment nearly always took precedence over preservation. To please park visitors, and to increase their numbers, Yellowstone superintendents allowed concessionaires to build hotels where views were best. (No matter that the choice spots happened to be only a hundred yards from the edge of Yellowstone Lake, or in the case of the Old Faithful Inn, nearly on top of a spectacular geyser.) They diverted hot springs to fill

bathing pools and stocked waters with non-native fishes. They built roads and trails where convenient. And they provided entertainment: bear-feeding shows at hotel dumps and light shows played across Old Faithful's evening eruptions.

Pleasing park visitors also meant keeping Yellowstone's animals in line, especially its "bad" animals. Wolves, cougars, and coyotes were considered a menace to "good" animals: elk and bighorn sheep, mule deer and pronghorn. So a formal extermination campaign was begun. Between 1904 and 1935, hunters and trappers killed 121 cougars, 136 wolves, and 4,352 coyotes.

To help favored species such as elk through bitter mountain winters, park keepers had hay pitched from feeding wagons during the early 1900s. In so doing, they foiled a culling process that had been at work for thousands of years.

The elk apparently thrived. So much so that park keepers feared a population irruption—and mass starvation. Picturing carcasses piling up on public highways and filling the backyards of nearby communities, superintendents reversed their tack. Beginning in the 1920s they established an elk removal program. By the next decade, they were corralling the animals in large numbers and either moving them to other ranges or killing them for meat, which they donated to Indian reservations.

From today's perspective, it is rather too easy to blame the park keepers for walking boot-shod over nature. The law that had established the National Park Service in 1916, though clearer and more sophisticated than Yellowstone's founding act, offered little management direction and much internal contradiction. The purpose of national parks, it said, was "to conserve the scenery and the natural and historic objects and the wild life therein and to provide for . . . enjoyment . . . by such means as will leave them unimpaired for . . . future generations."

To use yet preserve, to enjoy yet protect.

More often than not, things that went wrong were the result of someone's efforts to satisfy this contradictory mandate, someone responding to public and political pressure to enhance the natural setting, and—nearly always—someone acting on sketchy or false information.

Little was known about the relationship between animals and their environment before the 1940s. A stepchild among the sciences, ecology gained public recognition only gradually after World War II. The new science taught that all land and living things were woven into complex systems of interdependent parts. Wolves were part of that weave. So were humans—neither owners nor operators, said pioneer ecologist Aldo Leopold, but "fellow-voyageurs with other creatures in the odyssey of evolution." A whole different view of nature this was, suggesting the need for a different approach to wild lands: a "land ethic," said Leopold, affirming the right of plants, animals, soil, and water to "continued existence, and, at least in spots, their continued existence in a natural state."

The culling of elk at Yellowstone continued into the 1960s, when a newly informed public called for a halt to the practice. In response to the outcry, a special committee on wildlife management in the national parks produced a report in 1963 that was later adopted as park service policy. The report recommended that the park's natural features, as well as the forces that shaped those features, be maintained "or where necessary recreated, as nearly as possible in the condition that prevailed when the area was first visited by the white man. A national park should represent a vignette of primitive America."

National parks were important as reservoirs of our natural heritage, that ancient, still mysterious world that shaped and sustains life. The report criticized the park service for disturbing these reservoirs: for using pesticides, putting out wildfires, killing predators, and feeding wildlife. "Fed bears become bums, and dangerous. Fed elk deplete natural ranges. Forage relationships in wild animals should be natural."

Naturalness was the goal as long as it did not interfere with or destroy the idealistic portrait of primitive America. A few nettlesome realities troubled this notion. For one thing, not much was—or is—known about the natural state of national park regions when they were discovered. Perhaps more important, nature is not static. Plants and animals come and go; climate fluctuates. Park service officials debated: Should they manipulate a national park to preserve the ecological scene as viewed by the first European visitors, or should they allow it to wander, naturally, from that state?

From the report and the questions it raised came a startling new idea: that we let nature take its course in our national parks, let wild forces and processes dictate the future of wild lands. Unhindered by human interference, the system of natural checks and balances would work—if we took the long view and gave things time.

This hands-off philosophy, still in practice, led to a new definition of a park's value and purpose. "In Yellowstone the resource is not 20,000 elk, or a million lodgepole pines, or a grizzly bear," explains park ecologist Don Despain. "The resource is *wildness*. The interplay of all the parts of the wilderness—weather, animals, plants, earthquakes—acting upon each other . . . [creates] a state of existence, a wildness, that is the product and the resource for which Yellowstone is being preserved."

Nature managing nature. A simple idea. But are we willing to accept its consequences? Nature taking its course at Yellowstone is mountain pine beetles feeding on hundreds of acres of trees and wildfires reducing forests to black scars. It is bighorn sheep dying from pinkeye epidemics and elk herds reduced during harsh winters.

On the face these events seem messy, wasteful, and destructive. But Yellowstone has taught us: Traditional notions of good and bad, waste and destruction, do not hold in the wild. Take fire, for instance. If allowed to burn freely, wildfire clears out old and diseased trees and shrubs and accelerates the return of nutrients to soil. Even wildfires as widespread as those that swept through hundreds of thousands of acres at Yellowstone in the summer of 1988 can benefit vegetation and wildlife by generating vigorous new forest. Nearly 80 percent of Yellowstone's woodlands are lodgepole pine. This tall, slender tree has a type of pinecone that releases its seeds only in the heat of fire. Other species, too, thrive in the greater sunlight and reduced competition of those black scars. Long dormant plants bloom. Shrubs flourish, as do the birds and other wildlife they support. "Fire is a stimulant," says Yellowstone Superintendent Robert Barbee, "as important to the ecosystem as sunshine and rain."

Consider, also, the mountain pine beetle. By targeting older trees, the insects allow younger, healthy ones to flourish. Even a truly killing winter can serve the system by toughening elk herds through natural selection and by providing carrion for grizzlies, eagles, and other scavengers.

Not everyone, of course, holds with the theory of nonintervention. Some circles argue that the policy is slowly killing our parks, that Yellowstone, in particular, has been so radically transformed by the presence of humans that it can no longer function as a healthy ecosystem. We cannot afford to let wildfires burn or bighorn die from eye ailments. Just how wild can we allow our parks to be? The question is still hotly disputed.

On one matter most agree: The thorniest aspect of the national-park-as-ecosystem idea is the disparity between legal boundaries and biological ones. No park is big enough to function as a completely self-contained ecological unit. No park is an

Morning Glory Pool (left) was named for its likeness to the flower. Debris thrown by visitors has clogged the pool's vent, diminishing the flow of hot water. In cooler water yellow algae flourish, transforming the pool's original pure blue to blue-green.
   Viscous blobs of clay in a mud pot (above) hiss and bubble into mud flowers.

NEXT PAGES: Snow and steam whiten the Midway Geyser Basin, home to 12 of Yellowstone's 400 or so active geysers.

Michael D. Yandell

Dean Conger, National Geographic Staff (opposite); Michael H. Francis (below)

The Yellowstone River shines like quicksilver, beckoning anglers. Such trout-filled waters help support the park's grizzly bears. So do berries, grasses, and roots found in Yellowstone's forests and meadows—where the official park flower, the western fringed gentian (lower), blooms throughout the summer.

island. Yellowstone has taught us that, too.

The park's founders made the preserve a rectangle, large enough to include as yet undiscovered geological and scenic "curiosities," in case early explorers missed any (which they did—Yellowstone has some 10,000 geothermal features). The rectangle encloses a broad plateau, on average about a mile and a half in elevation, and high peaks that are snowbound in parts more than seven months a year. Its right-angled, straight-line boundaries run through mountain ranges, rivers, and valleys, with no regard for nature's seamless web of affairs.

Yellowstone's plants and animals make a mockery of these neat lines. Great herds of elk in search of winter grazing regularly migrate to lower lands across the park's northern border. Grizzly bears, mule deer, and bighorn sheep range beyond the boundaries in all directions. Put simply, the Yellowstone ecosystem is bigger than Yellowstone park—more than five times as big. Politically, the ecosystem is divided into two national parks, seven national forests, three wildlife refuges, and a small amount of other land. Ecologically, it is all of a piece. Bugs and bighorn do not stop at man-made boundaries. Neither do bears.

It was the grizzly bear that brought home this point at Yellowstone. Grizzly bears rely heavily on lands outside the park to forage for roots, berries, grasses, and other food. After the last of Yellowstone's open-pit garbage dumps were closed in the 1970s—part of the effort to restore the bears to a wild state—the average summer range of an adult male grizzly greatly increased as the bears readjusted to natural food sources. At least half of the home range for the 200 or so bears who survive today in the Yellowstone ecosystem lies outside park boundaries. Some of these areas are open to grazing and hunting, clear-cutting, road building, and recreational developments.

Grizzly bears need space and privacy. Without them, they die—often from fatal

Larry Ulrich

encounters with hunters, stockmen, land-owners, and automobiles. The grizzly's reproductive rate is very low. Even small changes in the number of reproducing adult females at Yellowstone can have a large impact on the population as a whole.

"Permanent grizzly ranges and permanent wilderness areas are of course two names for one problem," wrote Aldo Leopold more than four decades ago. Of late there has been some movement to address this problem with the founding in 1983 of an organization called the Interagency Grizzly Bear Committee (IGBC). The committee comprises representatives from federal land agencies and from the states of Idaho, Montana, Washington, and Wyoming. Its goal: To make management decisions about grizzly bears that take into consideration whole ecosystems, not just individual political segments.

The Greater Yellowstone Coalition, too, is committed to solving the problem of fragmented management in Yellowstone country. This federation of conservation groups and individuals seeks to promote understanding of the Yellowstone ecosystem and encourages cooperation among public agencies. Both the IGBC and the coalition have become models for other cooperative efforts to protect individual species and to preserve intact the ecosystems at Yellowstone and at parks around the world.

We are tinkerers, whether we like it or not. And the cardinal rule of the tinkerer, Leopold reminds us, is to keep all the pieces. Within a single park such as Yellowstone, that means preserving biological wholeness, sometimes by outright interference—restoring grizzly bear habitat, for instance, or reintroducing the gray wolf.

In the bigger picture, keeping all the pieces means preserving representative ecosystems—or at least samples of them. All but a handful of major ecosystems in the United States are now represented by national parks. Great Basin, established in

Elk bulls spar in a clearing before Castle Geyser. Yellowstone has one of the world's largest populations of elk—more than 30,000 in the summer, when the herds graze in park meadows and timber basins. In winter some herds move to lower lands outside Yellowstone. Others remain, providing spectacular wildlife viewing.

Cattle graze beneath the peaks of Nevada's Snake Range, the site of Great Basin National Park. Founded in 1986, Great Basin is the newest of the U.S. national parks. Its founding legislation permits ranchers to continue grazing cattle in perpetuity on parkland—a departure from usual national park legislation.

1986 as the newest national park, represents the Basin and Range Province, an immense expanse of land with high mountain ranges separated by broad valleys, and with no drainage to the sea.

Great Basin occupies a small chunk of high, lonely country in eastern Nevada. For those with roots deep in well-watered land, this is not an easy place to love, slighted as the empty home of sage and rabbit brush, pocket mouse and disappointment. But within Great Basin's space and silence there are cougars and bobcats. There are mule deer and bighorn, foxes, coyotes, and beavers. There are yellow-breasted chats and ruby-crowned kinglets. Violet-green swallows. Lazuli buntings. Golden eagles.

Through the heart of the park runs the Snake Range, with peaks as high as 13,000 feet. Valleys sprawl from the range on either side. A hike from valley to peak takes you from shadscale and sagebrush to piñon pine and juniper, then through forests of spruce, fir, and mountain mahogany thickly hung with green. On exposed ridges near tree line, you can find weathered bristlecone pines thousands of years old. And beyond, alpine meadows split with streams, and tundra speckled with hardy wildflowers.

Great Basin's boundaries include most of the major life zones found in the Basin and Range Province. Some skeptics argue that this is sheer luck. The park was founded for economic reasons, they say—specifically, to boost tourism in the nearby town of Ely and surrounding White Pine County. Ecosystem conservation was a happy by-product.

The park service brochure for Great Basin reads: "Don't be surprised to see cattle grazing in the park. The establishing legislation considers cattle grazing an integral part of the Great Basin scene. Similarly, unpatented mining claims may continue to be worked." It is hard to see how cattle and miners fit into a vignette of wild basin-and-range country. But the argument goes that the park would never have been founded

Great Basin National Park

120 Square Miles

Great Basin National Park is named for the geographic region it represents, a huge expanse of rugged mountain ranges and broad valleys that has no drainage to the sea. With elevations from 6,200 to 13,063 feet, the park contains most of the region's major life zones, from Upper Sonoran Desert to alpine tundra.

Wheeler Peak, Great Basin's highest mountain, harbors stands of bristlecone pine trees thousands of years old and a small glacier, one of the continent's southernmost permanent ice fields. Beneath the mountain's eastern flank is Lehman Caves—a network of limestone caverns filled with stalagmites, stalactites, flowstones, and thin mineral disks known as shields.

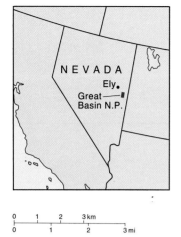

N E V A D A

Ely

Great Basin N.P.

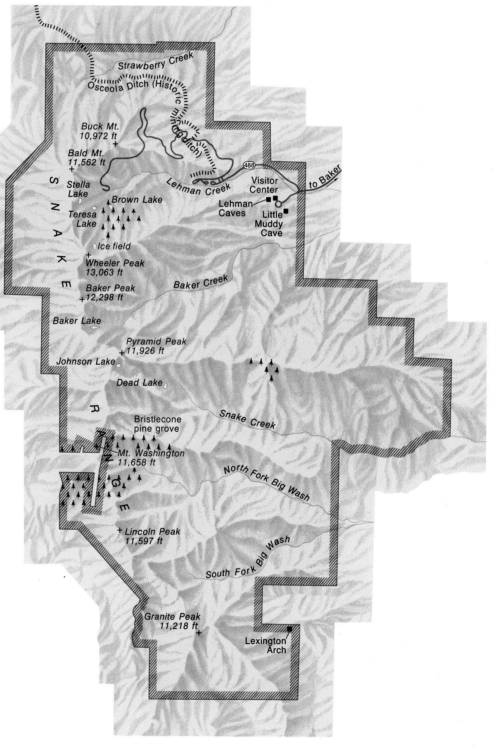

Strawberry Creek

Osceola Ditch (Historic mining ditch)

Buck Mt.
10,972 ft

Bald Mt.
11,562 ft

Lehman Creek

488

to Baker

Visitor Center

Stella Lake

Brown Lake

Lehman Caves

Little Muddy Cave

Teresa Lake

S N A K E

Ice field

Wheeler Peak
13,063 ft

Baker Peak
12,298 ft

Baker Creek

Baker Lake

Pyramid Peak
11,926 ft

Johnson Lake

Dead Lake

Snake Creek

R

Bristlecone pine grove

Mt. Washington
11,658 ft

North Fork Big Wash

G

E

Lincoln Peak
11,597 ft

South Fork Big Wash

Granite Peak
11,218 ft

Lexington Arch

Mule deer stop and stare before bolting. Named for the mule-like ears that help them detect danger at long range, mule deer live in Great Basin's mountainous areas. In winter they graze at lower elevations, returning to forage in alpine meadows with the onset of spring.

NEXT PAGES: Rock columns and shields festoon the limestone tunnels and galleries at Lehman Caves.

without these compromises.

Bills supporting a park in the Wheeler Peak area were proposed in the 1920s and again in the '50s and '60s, but defeated each time by Nevada ranching and mining interests. In 1985 the U.S. House of Representatives recommended establishing a Great Basin Park of 174,000 acres. Nevada senators countered with a bill for a 44,000-acre park, one that would, in the words of Senator Paul Laxalt, avoid "undue disruption of traditional mining and livestock activities." These activities, Laxalt said, are "as worthy of preservation in their own right as are the scenic features of the proposed Park." The compromise was a park $\frac{1}{30}$ the size of Yellowstone—77,000 acres, or 120 square miles—in which both grazing and mining may continue.

The park service has not yet settled on its plans for Great Basin. Some park enthusiasts would like to see new facilities developed. Others hope officials will expand only educational programs, not visitor centers and roads, following the counsel of Aldo Leopold: "Recreational development is a job not of building roads into lovely country, but of building receptivity into the still unlovely human mind."

Once the park service determines its strategy for developing Great Basin, it will proceed only after careful study of the park's wildlife and vegetation. It has, one hopes, learned some lessons from controversies surrounding Yellowstone's facilities—Fishing Bridge, in particular, a complex of two campgrounds, a store, gas station, museum, and other buildings sitting astride some of the park's most important grizzly bear habitat. Though many conservationists and park service researchers agree that Fishing Bridge threatens the grizzly bear and other Yellowstone wildlife, the drive to remove the development has been stalled by powerful commercial and pro-recreation interest groups.

The national park idea has moved away from its utilitarian, recreational beginnings, but its philosophical foundations remain shaky. If, in compromises at Great Basin and Yellowstone, we seem to stray from the goals of naturalness and conservation of biological wholeness, it is because we are still torn by the two powerful and opposing drives of the park service mandate—to use and yet preserve. We cannot, perhaps, join these two successfully. But something good or even great can result from the attempt of a people to reconcile them, keeping in mind the ideal of wildness and the aim of gentle, knowing stewardship.

By Jennifer Gorham Ackerman
Photographs by Jim Brandenburg

High on Wheeler Peak grow hardy conifers (right), including the ancient bristlecone pine. *Pinus longaeva* is one of the longest lived organisms known. Its resinous, rot-resistant wood helps it survive storms and periods of drought. Shorter lived but more abundant is the piñon pine (above), here growing near rimrock cliffs.

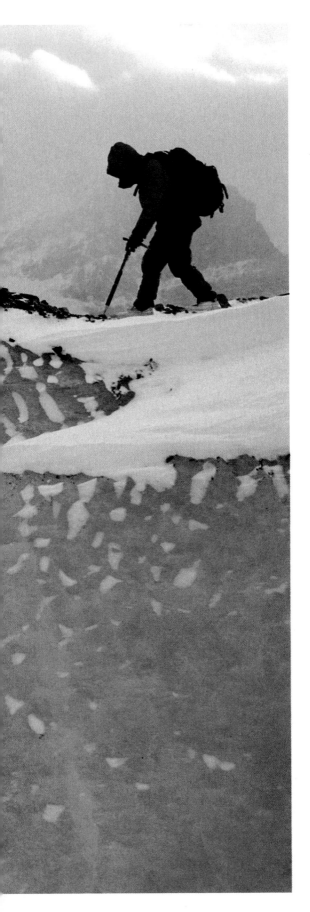

Where perennial winter clings to the land, a climber picks his way across the Athabasca Glacier. This tongue of ice, more than three miles long, reaches down from the Continental Divide and into Jasper National Park, largest in Canada's Rockies.

A Race with the Season

It was drizzling that November day when we turned our horses north into the Canadian Rockies and formed a single column: a rider leading a packhorse by a length of rope, another rider, and another rider leading a packhorse. We crossed and recrossed Stoney Creek, and as the afternoon lengthened, the trail climbed beyond the tree line. The drizzle turned to spitting snow of the sort that makes your flesh creep when it clings to your neck and melts there. By dusk the wind was screeching. It whipped the snow into dervishes, and it bombarded us with tiny ice bullets, thousands of them that stung our faces, numbed our ears, and limited visibility to a few feet.

"I sort of miss the flies."

The voice belonged to Frank Burstrom, a ghostly form riding ahead of me. It is the only thing I remember him saying all afternoon. Burstrom, a warden who works for Banff National Park, has a documented hatred for flies, from a slow day in August when he killed exactly 226 of them in a secluded cabin. He methodically recorded the slaughter in a logbook, which hangs by a loop of twine on the cabin wall.

Now, with this foretaste of winter, even Burstrom thought fondly of flies. Most of the green had faded from the high meadows, where lichens provided the only color —splotches of orange and yellow on gray rocks the wind had swept clean of snow. Burstrom tilted his Stetson so that it shielded his face from the wind.

It was still the shoulder of the season, neither autumn nor winter, in the four contiguous national parks of the Canadian Rockies. These mountain parks—Banff, Jasper, Yoho, and Kootenay—cover some

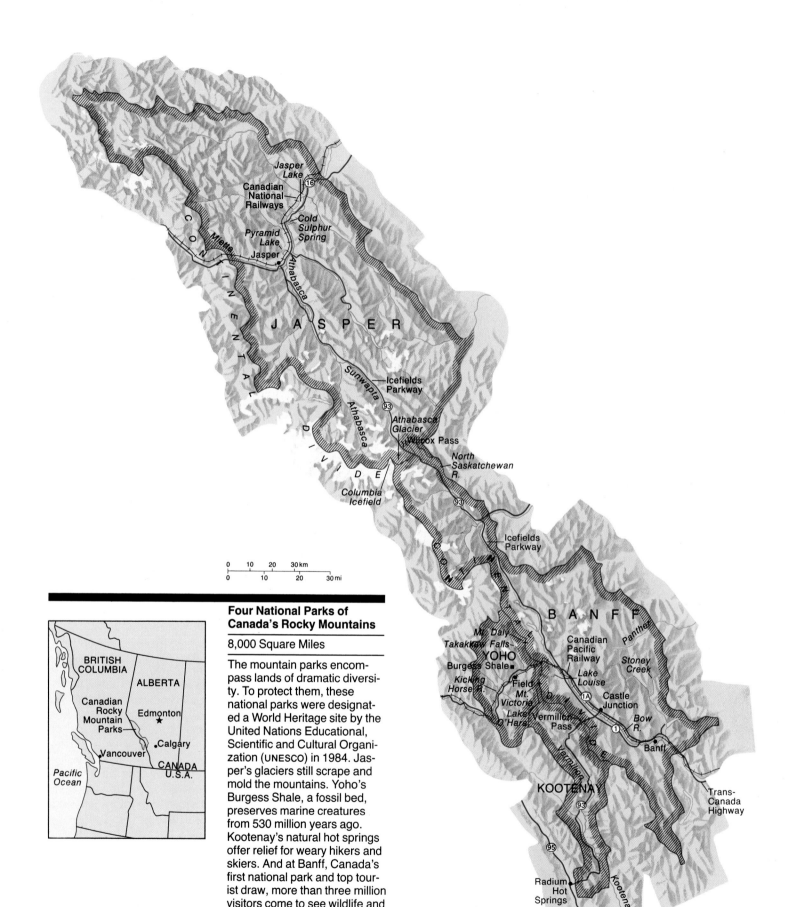

Jasper Lake

Canadian National Railways

Cold Sulphur Spring

Pyramid Lake

Jasper

Athabasca

JASPER

CONTINENTAL

Miette

DIVIDE

Sunwapta

Icefields Parkway

Athabasca

Athabasca Glacier

Wilcox Pass

North Saskatchewan R.

Columbia Icefield

Icefields Parkway

CONTINENTAL

BANFF

Panther

Mt. Daly

Takakkaw Falls

Canadian Pacific Railway

Stoney Creek

YOHO

Burgess Shale

Kicking Horse R.

Field

Mt. Victoria

Lake Louise

Lake O'Hara

Vermilion Pass

Castle Junction

Bow R.

Banff

Vermilion

KOOTENAY

Trans-Canada Highway

Kootenay

Radium Hot Springs

Four National Parks of Canada's Rocky Mountains

8,000 Square Miles

The mountain parks encompass lands of dramatic diversity. To protect them, these national parks were designated a World Heritage site by the United Nations Educational, Scientific and Cultural Organization (UNESCO) in 1984. Jasper's glaciers still scrape and mold the mountains. Yoho's Burgess Shale, a fossil bed, preserves marine creatures from 530 million years ago. Kootenay's natural hot springs offer relief for weary hikers and skiers. And at Banff, Canada's first national park and top tourist draw, more than three million visitors come to see wildlife and other attractions each year.

BRITISH COLUMBIA

ALBERTA

Canadian Rocky Mountain Parks

Edmonton

Calgary

Vancouver

CANADA U.S.A.

Pacific Ocean

Like a storybook castle, the Banff Springs Hotel towers above the spruces in Banff National Park. Scores of elk gather to breed on the hotel's lush golf course each autumn. "Other golf courses only have water hazards," says Ivor Petrak, general manager and vice president of the hotel. "Here, we have elk hazards."

8,000 square miles. Each year more than nine million people visit these parks, the most popular in Canada, but you would never guess it on this day.

The summer tourists had fled weeks ago, along with the warblers, black swifts, Canada geese, and other seasonal visitors. Now the mountains belonged to the hardiest residents—the grizzlies, hoary marmots, ground squirrels, and western jumping mice that would drowse through the months ahead to conserve energy, out of sight. Other year-rounders would face winter head-on: elk and cougars, bighorn sheep and gray wolves, moose and ravens, gray jays and red squirrels, mountain goats and American dippers, snowshoe hares and wolverines. Each was a specialist. The wolves and cougars, for example, were expert at killing; the wolverines and ravens, at scavenging what the killers left behind; the dippers, at finding open streams where they could snatch nymphs from subsurface stones. Day after day would bring subzero temperatures, and winter could bring five feet of snow. In a race with the season, many of the animals would breed now so that their young could arrive with the spring. Food would be more plentiful then.

The wardens, too, were driven by the seasons. Frank Burstrom and his partner, Larry Gilmar, were riding their last horse patrol of the year. Next time they entered the backcountry, it would be on skis. They moved when the bighorns did, watched for signs that the bears were denning up, searched the hills for wolf dens, followed the elk down the valleys as the days began to shorten. Our packhorses carried enough food and extra clothing for four days, the time it would take to ride 50 or 60 miles of the backcountry. We would look for horse tracks and human footprints in the snow, for it was hunting season and people sometimes sneaked across the park boundary to shoot wildlife.

"We seldom catch them in the act of

Lake Louise reflects the ice-bound hulk of Mount Victoria. Bands of limestone in the mountaintop, where snow clings in layers, reveal Victoria's former status as a seabed. The lake, fed by meltwater, owes its translucent green color to fine particles of rock, ground by glaciers and suspended in the icy water.

Tom Algire

poaching," said Gilmar, "but we want them to know we're around, checking up on things. Keeps the beggars honest."

We rode through the high country for five hours, then descended toward the park's eastern boundary. The snow diminished as we lost altitude, and we passed into the gathering darkness, down through the bare willows, down through the fragrant firs, down, finally, to a one-room warden's cabin where we would spend the night.

It looked inviting enough until I saw the welcome mat, a three-by-four-foot board with row upon row of three-inch nails driven through it, points up, in front of the door.

"Keeps the grizzlies out," said Gilmar. "They break in to get food, and they trash the place. They're hibernating now." He paused. "Probably." Gilmar smiled.

Next day the weather cleared. We rode through grizzly country, up and down the mountains, in and out of shadow, through deep valleys hardly wider than a horse's width. Elk skulls, leg bones, and broken bits of skeletons littered the meadows, but not a bear stirred. We looped out of the park to visit hunters whose tent camps clustered just beyond the boundary. They waited for the season's first big snow, one that would push the elk down from the protection of the park and into their gunsights.

"Better for a picnic than for hunting." The speaker was a white-bearded hunting guide with slicked-back hair and plaid flannel slippers. We lounged by the stove in his tent, drinking his coffee and eating his homemade cookies. Sitting with us were a surgeon and an anesthesiologist, up from the States for a week. One of the sports wore a camouflage undershirt and a compass on a string that hung down his chest like a pendant. He looked glum. All dressed up, nothing to shoot. Beyond the open tent flaps snow lay sprinkled, thin as talcum powder, on the frozen ground. "The horses should be belly deep in snow by now," sniffed the guide. "Nobody's getting anything."

The wardens believed him. Finding no signs of poaching or rumors of it, we turned back into the park. Winter held off, the elk stayed out of reach, and three days passed before we saw the first one.

It was worth the wait. He was a bull of perhaps a thousand pounds, a magnificent specimen that seemed to know it. He walked from the dark woods at a regal pace and eased down the bank into the Panther River. He stopped at midstream and stood there, as if to pose, and showed us a heavy set of antlers, seven points to a side, which swooped above his head. He nosed the water at his leisure, waded across, and emerged in the morning sunlight. His dark mane and belly dripped with water from the river as he calmly lifted his head to watch us, the intruders in his meadow. He resumed grazing, as if to say we did not matter to him, not at all.

Seeing such an animal on this calm morning, one was tempted to rhapsodize about the elk of Banff National Park being in residence for thousands of years without interruption, now as ever before. In truth, however, almost all the elk had vanished from the Canadian Rockies by the turn of this century, their numbers decimated by diminishing habitat and overhunting. To restore the herds in Banff and Jasper parks, more than 250 elk were imported from Yellowstone National Park between 1917 and 1920. They thrived in their new home, where more than 3,500 live today.

The bull we had seen was all alone. Most likely he was resting from the rigors of the breeding season just past, the frenzied weeks of autumn when males lose their appetite and begin to behave in a bizarre manner. They scrape their antlers on trees, they cough and make strange grunting sounds in the night, they urinate in the dirt and roll in it. Some walk 60 miles to challenge other bulls and gather their own harems. Antlers, grown and discarded each year, are an advertisement, emblem of the owner's health.

If a bull has eaten well, his antlers flourish; if not, they look thin and pathetic, announcing his lack of success to all prospective mates. When males of comparable size fight, they lock antlers and shove each other around in circles until one proves his supremacy. The winner, the fellow with the best constitution, attracts females; his harem may number 15 strong. The top bull breeds with them all, while watching for competitors that try to impregnate his cows on the sly. It is hard, dangerous work.

As the rutting season dwindles, bulls may develop a fever because they are covered with wounds, with an average of 45 battle scrapes, gouges, cuts. Sometimes they lose an eye. The cows, by contrast, spend less energy in the rut and so have more reserves to draw upon, for themselves and their embryonic calves, in the harsh months ahead.

The elk's season was on the wane. But the bighorn sheep were just starting their own spectacular breeding rituals, so I left Banff and drove north to Jasper National Park to watch them.

The route to Jasper, along the Icefields Parkway, passes through a ravaged landscape. It has been tilted and ripped by continental forces, chiseled by ice, smoothed and torn again by water and wind. Perpetual ice, in some places 1,500 feet thick, still covers some 550 square miles of the Canadian Rockies. The mountains look tortured here, grand and immutable there, here rising like a monstrous ocean wave on the upswing, frozen in the instant before it uncurls.

The oceanic image comes to mind when you climb all morning, reach a summit and find, there under your boot a mile above sea level, the delicate outline of a cephalopod, a squidlike mollusk that swam in warm seas more than 350 million years ago. You bend to trace the fossil with your finger and feel the animal's cold imprint in the Devonian limestone, and suddenly your mind races forward across the ages. Will human remains last as long?

The huge silence of the Rockies, which grows as the days shrink, prompts such thoughts of mortality. But this is also a time for regeneration, which starts the bighorn rams on their seasonal journeys.

A group of three rams, with their distinctive curling horns and chocolate brown coats, trotted beside the road, heading north. They moved at a steady clip in single file, with a seeming sense of urgency.

"Look at them. Hog fat! Hog fat! Just rolling in fat! Nice big fat wide buns!"

Valerius Geist was speaking, in exclamation marks as usual, as we watched the rams through binoculars. A professor at the University of Calgary, Geist has the teacher's knack for infecting others with his own enthusiasm and for repeating things in an interesting way. I got the point: The rams carried extra fat just now because they would feed little in the weeks to come, concentrating their energies on traveling, head bashing, and breeding.

For some 30 years Geist has studied mountain sheep and other ruminants. He has been treed by a grizzly, chased by several bull moose, and hit by a 250-pound ram. To get closer to some mountain goats, Geist disguised himself as one, pulling on white coveralls, wrapping his head in a white towel, creeping on all fours along a narrow ledge of rock. It worked. The goats tolerated him. Geist likes to see his animals up close, and now he was introducing me to them.

"See that big one?" said Geist, referring to a ram. "His testes are hanging out nicely. That's important. That shows he's been eating well. He will need all of that sperm. These rascals will lead us to where the girls are. That's where they're going!"

We followed, got too close, and sent them scattering. It was hopeless to catch up, so we pressed northward again, this time to Wilcox Pass, a part of Jasper park where migrating sheep often converge in November. We climbed a worn path through a meadow. Judging from the abundance of scat and hoofprints, it was a sheep highway. We swept the frozen hills with our binoculars, looking for signs of movement. More than an hour passed before we found, a mile and a half in the distance, some blobs of brown against a yellow background of grass: a mixed group including one ram, three ewes, two lambs, and a yearling. All grazed except for the big ram. He dozed, draped over an outcrop in the sun.

Geist began the approach. "Hello, lady! Hello! Hello!" he shouted into the cold air. A cheery voice. Geist waved at the nearest ewe, like a flagman trying to stop a train. All the sheep, except for the napping ram, snapped to attention. Geist waved again, yelled again, and we approached a few steps. The sheep resumed grazing. We edged closer. How did it work?

"It works because we're not acting the role of carnivores," said Geist, kicking at the grass as a sheep would. "A wolf goes for them in a straight line or tries to hide. We're zigzagging. You have to pause. Look at the sky. Act as if you have all the time in the world. Stay in their field of vision. What predator would behave that way?"

We finally got so close that our binoculars were useless. The big ram awoke, approached a ewe, and smelled her rear. Then he raised his head and seemed to smile, curling his lips so that his teeth and gums were visible. At the moment of that lip curl, a specialized bundle of tissues called the Jacobson's organ was at work in the roof of the ram's mouth, measuring hormones in the ewe's urine. If the ewe was in heat, the Jacobson's organ would tell the ram.

She was not. Our ram licked his lips and went on to check the next ewe and the next. Then, having established that they were not ready, he wandered off. He walked up through the meadow, paused to scan the horizon, grazed a bit, walked again. He stopped and searched the mountains.

"A sheep alone," said Geist, "is not a happy sheep. He's looking for another group."

A quartet of bighorn sheep gathers before Mount Aeolus in Jasper National Park. When resting, the group arranges itself so that each sheep avoids eye contact with any other; a direct stare could be taken as a sign of aggression, prompting retribution from a dominant member of the group.

A fierce wind rose from the Athabasca Glacier, still visible to the west. The wind gathered up the glacier's cold and flung it down across the meadow. We were frozen, about to leave, when another ram trotted into view. He was the very image of the fellow we had been trailing—perhaps 250 pounds, seven years old, primed for the rut.

He spotted our ram and stopped in his tracks. He watched.

"He's getting an eyeful!" said Geist. "Oh boy! We could have some butting heads!"

Geist turned to watch our ram, now sleeping. "Come on, Mr. Chickenheart! Get up!"

The Stranger came closer. Chickenheart dreamed on. The Stranger approached, 800 feet, 500 feet, 300 feet nearer. When the Stranger was within 100 feet, Chickenheart stood to face him. Each stretched his neck and rolled his eyes until the whites showed. Each lifted his head, displaying his horns to full advantage.

"Fireworks!" said Geist.

The Stranger closed in. He kicked Chickenheart in the chest. It was a tap delivered with a front leg.

"Fireworks!" said Geist. "He's calling Mr. Chickenheart a girl! Insulting him! The gauntlet is thrown!"

Chickenheart made his move.

He stepped up to the Stranger and nuzzled him under the eye like a pussycat trying to make friends.

"That's it! Finito! Boy, did he cave in!" It was Geist again. The moment Chickenheart had nuzzled the Stranger, he had taken on the smell of the dominant ram from the Stranger's preorbital gland. Wherever Chickenheart went now, he would smell like one of the Stranger's subordinates.

This time of year, one ram tolerates another only if the other behaves as a ewe, thus posing no threat to the ram's breeding agenda. Sometimes the tougher ram will even mount a subordinate to show his dominance. If two rams of comparable size meet and one does not submit, the contest may

When winter comes to the Rockies, bighorn sheep converge on their breeding grounds. Rams curl their lips (left) after sniff-testing a ewe's readiness for breeding. One kicks another in a dominance display (lower left). Such insults may escalate into clashing (right), from which one victor eventually emerges to mate with all available ewes.

escalate. One insults the other, the insult is returned, and they butt heads until a victor emerges. The fight can last more than 25 hours. In sheep society as in elk society, the top stud gets breeding privileges with the females and passes the flock's genetic strength to the next generation.

It was almost night at Wilcox Pass when the rams finally parted company. We found our way back to the car in the dark. We had a long drive that night, and Geist regaled me with stories of bears and fishing trips, of wardens and outlaws, including one about a poacher who sometimes slept on the roof, just for the heck of it. It was a sloping roof.

"If a national park can't produce characters, what good is it?" asked Geist.

Did the parks produce them still? "Yes, there are young characters just growing into the role. For the same reasons. Solitude! Harsh conditions! They force you to rely on your own wits, and that makes for independent people."

Those words came back to me a few days later, when I met Ben Gadd in the little town of Jasper, the headquarters for Jasper National Park. Gadd, trained as a geologist, once worked as a park naturalist, then gave it up to become a writer and nature guide.

He spends his days hiking, identifying plants, inspecting rocks, looking at ravens. A park superintendent recently described him as "one of the puristic bug-and-bunny boys," a label Gadd happily embraced.

"If it were not for the bugs," Gadd once wrote, "the wildflowers wouldn't get pollinated, and we mountain dwellers would be up to our navels in unprocessed elk poop." Gadd was full of surprises like that. We were sitting in his house one night, chatting about wolves, when Gadd suddenly stood and made this suggestion:

"Let's go for a howl. I haven't howled since last fall."

It was late, but we bundled up, grabbed our hats, piled into Gadd's rusty Subaru wagon, and went for a howl. We headed for

Jasper Lake, braided with silt and sand from the Atha-basca River, shrinks to a shadow of itself in winter. Then westerly winds gather up the exposed sediment and deposit sand in great heaps along the shore, form-ing a most unexpected sight in the Canadian Rockies— sand dunes. Some rise to a hundred feet.

NEXT PAGES: A river of glacial ice flows from the Columbia Icefield, which covers some 125 square miles of Cana-da's Rockies.

Jim Brandenburg

A climber inches up a frozen waterfall in Yoho National Park. Climbers jab their way along with ice axes; crampons—metal spikes lashed to boots—provide a toehold in the icicles. Hundreds of ice climbers challenge the Rockies' crags and canyons each winter, which is also a time for skating, skiing, sledding, and other sports.

Pyramid Lake, a regular staging area for wolves. They gather here to hunt in winter, usually seven or eight to the pack. One wolf announces himself with a howl, and another answers. That prompts a chorus of howls, and the night fills up with strange music. The pack coalesces around a dominant male that guides the group in search of elk, sheep, and the occasional moose. While the pack hunts, an older brother may stay behind to baby-sit the pups of the year.

We stumbled around the shore, found a footbridge, followed it over an end of the lake, and stopped halfway across. Gadd cupped his hands and howled like a master. It started as a low rumbling in his chest, elevated to a growl, and advanced to a blood-curdling wail that stood my hair on end. We waited for an answer. Nothing. Gadd tried again and again, but no answer came, only the sound of waves slapping the beach and the wind sawing through the pines.

"Too rough for a decent howl," Gadd concluded, so we called it a night.

Our luck changed the next day. We chanced upon a pair of wolves at work along the Miette River, where a grove of aspens closed tight around a towering white spruce. The wolves, crouching when we first spotted them, looked up. They regarded us with cold yellow eyes. We stood stock-still. One wolf was black, the other gray—probably mates for life. They sniffed the ground once more, glanced our way, then slipped off, now hardly more than shadows traveling close to the ground. They moved through the trees, gained a hill, and melted from view. They did not look back.

We went to see where they had been digging. Gadd pointed to a bed of flattened leaves, probably where a deer or elk had curled up for a nap. What did the wolves smell there? Had the sleeper left behind some sign of weakness? A fever that produced more sweat than usual? Odors that could tell of wounds or sickness? No one knows for sure, but something had drawn the wolves here. Perhaps they would follow this animal, drive it into the open, run it to exhaustion, perhaps cripple it. They would kill by ripping open the victim's belly or by closing their jaws over its windpipe. They would eat their fill, first the nutrient-rich organs, then whatever meat they still had room for. Then they would find a quiet place to sleep off the meal. When they woke again, they would return to pick at the carcass. A pack needed to kill an elk or its equivalent every three days or so. Death was a way of life here.

Perhaps our pair of wolves was investigating another bed now, just over the hill. We followed but could not find them. When we stopped, silence spread through the woods. Not a leaf turned, not a twig crackled for miles and miles. "They're probably watching us now," Gadd whispered.

Until quite recently wolves were unwelcome here. Wardens shot them, ranchers and fur trappers in the provinces poisoned them. By the early 1950s, wolves had virtually disappeared. Although no wolves have been reintroduced in the mountain parks, their numbers are climbing, mirroring a growth in the population of elk, their primary prey. Some 90 wolves spend at least part of the year in Jasper park, about 30 in Banff park. Because they are hunters, they need a huge range: A pack may cover a hundred-mile circuit several times a month. The parks are their sanctuary.

"We're happy the wolves are coming back," said John G. Woods, a zoologist who works in the mountain parks. "We hope that natural forces, such as the wolves, will soon be the leading cause of death in elk here—ahead of cars and trains."

Hundreds of animals, mainly elk, deer, moose, and bighorn sheep, are lost to cars and trains each year. A six-million-dollar fencing program in Banff National Park reduced highway kills of elk—from fifty-five to one—in the first year of the project. Park officials may add miles of new fencing.

Naturalist Ben Gadd explores a cave in the Athabasca Glacier (above). Inside, bubbles and grit in a slab of ice show the direction of the glacier's movement (right). Two centuries may pass as a single snowflake cycles through: It settles on the glacier's head, compacts there, and finally emerges as meltwater from the glacier's toe.

NEXT PAGES: Snow swirls over the Continental Divide, where the ice is 1,500 feet thick in places.

From the start, Canada's mountain parks were linked with major transportation arteries, first the Canadian Pacific Railway, then later the Canadian National Railways and the Trans-Canada Highway.

Two railroad hands, helping to build the first line through the Rockies, came upon hot springs in 1883, near what is now the town of Banff, and in 1885 the government designated the area as Banff Hot Spring Reserve for "the sanitary advantage of the public." The reserve was soon expanded to 260 square miles and named the Rocky Mountains Park. It was Canada's first national park, later renamed Banff. Yoho was the next park established, in 1886, followed by Jasper in 1907 and Kootenay in 1920.

One who lobbied for Canada's first park was William C. Van Horne, an energetic Yankee and general superintendent of the Canadian Pacific Railway. "If we can't export the scenery, we'll import the tourists!" he said, and set out to promote the Canadian Rockies as the "mountain playground of the world." He brought rich customers across Canada to explore the mountains, to soak in the hot sulfurous pools, and to stay in the Banff Springs Hotel, a château the railroad had built. Visitors traveled in the comfort of parlor cars, dined on fine food, and used the hotel as a base for touring. Suddenly the wilderness was accessible.

"Magnificent mountains before and around me, their lofty peaks smiling down on us, and never a frown on their grand faces!" The writer was Lady Agnes Macdonald; the year, 1886. She was crossing the Continental Divide on the newly finished Canadian Pacific Railway, describing the scene from an unusual vantage point—the cowcatcher of Engine 374.

More than a century later, the cowcatchers are gone, but modern travelers can still cross the Divide by rail and see, as Lady Agnes did, those "lofty forests, dark and deep" in Yoho National Park.

I took the afternoon train from Banff,

northwest through the wall of mountains. With the evening, snow began to fall. We reached the summit, and the train slid down the pass into Yoho. Five or six elk bounded into a forest of Engelmann spruce, where snow made the branches droop. The engine slowed and stopped. We waited for an eastbound train to come through a tunnel. Two girls played cards across the aisle, and a fellow from Australia talked about the dust-blown hills at home, and we glanced up now and then to watch the snow pile up outside. The light from our coach cast a thin sheen of yellow on the snow, which was drifted and scalloped like sand dunes.

The heavy snows arrive first on the western side of the Rockies. Air masses gather moisture over the Pacific Ocean, then blow eastward, reach the mountain barrier, and begin to climb it. As the air rises and cools, its moisture condenses, forming clouds that produce snow in the winter, rain in the summer—a process known as orographic lifting. Much of the moisture is wrung out as the air crosses the mountains—one reason the eastern parks, Banff and Jasper, are drier than the western, Kootenay and Yoho.

"We've had three park visitors in the past week. Everybody's getting a little depressed," said Harry Abbott, a young warden at Yoho. It was almost Thanksgiving, and he had a case of cabin fever. Like other mountain dwellers, Abbott had endured the gray weeks of October and early November, when it was too late for hiking and too early for skiing. He had been waiting for this snow and the first ski trip of the season, an eight-mile journey to Lake O'Hara.

We skied all morning, following a roadbed that climbed through silent woods and arched over half-frozen creeks, where cascading water spilled back upon itself to form ice clouds between the banks. I led the way at first but soon asked Abbott to go ahead. I did not want to hold him back. He disappeared around a bend, and I relished the solitude, gliding at my own pace, listening to the long swish of my skis in the new powder, watching the wolverine tracks weave on and off the trail, stopping now and then to hear my own heart pounding in my ears. When that internal racket subsided, the quiet was such that you could hear each snowflake brushing through the trees, settling in the woods, touching your face.

By afternoon Abbott and I reached the lake. It was frozen, carpeted in snow. We skied across it, with jagged mountains rising all around, and it was dark when we finished exploring that evening.

The next day, just as we prepared to ski back down, I heard the nasal *wheeoo* of a gray jay. I turned toward the sound and held out my hand. The smoky gray bird swooped out of the woods, buzzed my hand, shot into another tree. It watched me. It flew my way again and landed on my finger. Its grip was delicate but firm, a jaunty bird with shifty black eyes. The jay cocked its head again, first one way, then another, and saw that I had no food. So much for me. A fluttering of wings and it disappeared in the trees. Its companions chattered there, but none came over to investigate.

Gray jays, among the boldest and most abundant of the birds here, travel under a range of aliases: camp robbers, Canada jays, whiskey jacks—the last an anglicized version of their Cree name, *wiskatjon*. Supremely opportunistic, they eat almost anything: carrion, bugs, berries, nestlings, bits of tourists' sandwiches. They hoard food in autumn, coating it with sticky saliva that may contain an antibacterial agent. The food, hidden in tree cavities and wedged under bark, is stashed away for winter use and as emergency rations for nestlings, which hatch long before other species. Thus do young jays get a head start on all the others.

Winter was closing fast now. Abbott and I skied down from Lake O'Hara in a fine snow that drifted over our tracks from the day before. By Christmas this empty trail would fill with tourists headed for lodges

Wardens practice an aerial rescue in Yoho National Park. Tethered to a helicopter, the rescuers arrive (opposite). They strap the victim into an aluminum frame (above left) and pack him into a cocoon-like Jenny bag. The aircraft takes the victim and rescuer to safety (above), then returns for the remaining passenger.

scattered around the backcountry.

My time was almost done. I drove down to the last park, Kootenay, where I hoped to see the bighorn sheep finish their season. I had heard that they were finally bashing heads there. I found rams snorting at each other, rams chasing ewes through the trees, ewes giving rams the slip, rams kicking each other at both ends. Day by day the tension built, but the finale never came. Each day was shorter, colder than the one before. I began calling the other parks to see what other rams were up to, and on the night before Thanksgiving, heard what I wanted from Wes Bradford, a warden at Jasper:

"They're cracking heads up here," he said.

"Should I drive up?"

"You probably should."

So I abandoned Kootenay and headed north toward Jasper: crossed the Divide at Vermilion Pass, turned north from Castle Junction, then raced along the Icefields Parkway. In passing, I saw coyotes hunting in the grass, a cow moose ruminating in the shadows, blue glacial ice glowing on the mountains, but I barely noticed. The sheep beckoned. Bradford's directions led me to a place called Cold Sulphur Spring, where a few threads of water trickle from dolomite cliffs, making the air stink of rotten eggs.

The sheep were there, a group of small rams and ewes gathered on one side of the road, three huge rams on the other. I shut off the engine. They grazed. I was making

notes when the first clash came, so I did not see it. But the sound was unmistakable, like two bowling balls slammed together.

Two of the rams prepared for another clash: They turned from each other, walked eight or ten paces, and swiveled around. Eyes wide, ears flat, each sighted the other. They stood on their hind legs, poised a moment in the air, and charged. *Clack!* They did it again. *Clack!* And again. *Clack!* Each time they staggered with the blow, wheeled, and crashed again. It lasted no more than five minutes, with two clashing and one watching. Occasionally the three rams huddled, nose to nose to nose, and compared horns. It ended as suddenly as it had started. The rams resumed grazing as if nothing

had happened. Then the big rams began clashing again. This time they took turns, first one, then another, challenging the third one. The defender's horn tips, broken and splintered, spoke of his stormy past; a previous fight had chiseled a triangular chip from his right horn. He became Chips in my notebook, so I could tell him from the others. Chips held his own, meeting each challenge, turning to face the next one, making an opponent wince after one clash.

This second round of clashes lasted no more than ten minutes. It ended about sundown, but I could not say who won. Perhaps the score would be settled later. Chips crossed the road, sniffed at each grazing ewe, and found that they were not ready

Harry Abbott, a warden in Yoho National Park, dips water for cooking and washing from the Yoho River. Wardens patrol the backcountry by horse or on skis, and stay in cabins dotted throughout the four mountain parks. At the Takakkaw Falls cabin, Abbott shovels the porch to start his day.

to breed. He wandered westward, toward Jasper townsite. The others watched him go. His breath made coils of steam in the dim light. He looked back, stooped to lick salt from the road, and resumed his journey, fat sides jiggling as he trotted away.

That night I wondered where Chips was going, what would await him, if he would prevail this year. A few days passed and I forgot him. December opened with a hard freeze. One brilliant morning I stopped to watch a flock of 20 ravens circling over the railroad tracks outside the town of Jasper. They dropped around the bend, out of sight. A bald eagle soared over, turned back, and landed in a treetop. He watched the tracks too. Then came a black wolf, loping down to the rails. Something had died.

I climbed a slope to the railbed and followed the curving steel. The wolf looked awful: emaciated, with all the fur gone from his back. Perhaps it was mange. He would not likely survive the winter. My approach sent the scavengers scrambling—ravens to the sky, wolf to the woods. Only the eagle remained, safe on his perch.

All had been feasting on a ram. Maybe he was one I had seen clashing before. It was hard to tell for sure, because he had been hit by a train. Then the scavengers had gone to work on him. His eyes were gone, his belly was opened and stripped of organs, his back legs were gnawed to the bones. One horn lay ten feet from the other. I lifted it, turned it in my hands. It was heavy. I counted the growth rings. He had lived eight years. I laid his horn in the cinders again and left.

The eagle stayed and the ravens circled on and on. The wolf was gone. I followed the rails, rounded the curve, and noticed some sheep grazing on the mountainside. I lifted my binoculars: Chips. There was no mistaking the old rascal, napping in the sun, surrounded by ewes, with one less rival to worry about this winter noon.

By Robert M. Poole
Photographs by James Balog

Triggered by a warden's bomb, a controlled avalanche rumbles through the spruces in Kootenay National Park. Where avalanches constantly threaten public safety, wardens perform regular snow surveys, digging through several layers to make a microscopic analysis of snow (above). When slides are likely, park authorities set off avalanches to forestall danger.

Africa

Most of us, in our imaginations, inhabit an Africa that no longer exists. It is the Africa of Isak Dinesen's Ngong Hills, Hemingway's green hills, Conrad's heart of darkness, Burton's Nile. In the past two decades that Africa has almost vanished.

"The chief feature of the landscape, and of your life in it, was the air," Dinesen wrote in *Out of Africa* in 1937. "Looking back on a sojourn in the African highlands, you are struck by your feeling of having lived for a time up in the air. The sky was rarely more than pale blue or violet, with a profusion of mighty, weightless, ever-changing clouds towering up and sailing on it, but it has a blue vigour in it. . . . Up in this high air you breathed easily, drawing a vital assurance and lightness of heart."

In July of 1982 a vast cloud of hot dust from the Sahara—a front of air pollution a thousand miles long—drifted across the Atlantic and settled over most of Florida. *That* is the sort of air coming out of Africa these days. North Africa has lost 270,000 square miles to "desert creep" in the past 50 years. After desertification and drought in the Sahara and the Sahel comes famine. A generation ago Ethiopia and Sudan were magically evocative names. Today they evoke civil war, swollen bellies, and malnutrition.

Economic disaster, political entropy, and automatic weapons have spread to nearly every corner of the continent. Of the 65,000 black rhinos inhabiting southern, central, and eastern Africa 15 years ago, more than 90 percent have been killed. The black rhino is extinct or on the verge of extinction in the Sudan, Uganda, Chad. The elephant is nearly extinct in Somalia. There is little ivory left in the Ivory Coast, nothing but a few relict elephant herds.

The older Africa, that Africa of our imaginations, survives only in parks. But the parks, too, are troubled places. Rampant poaching is the great problem.

In the early 1970s the military rule of Idi Amin ruined Uganda's economy, its tourist industry, and it

---

Tanzania

**Ngorongoro
Conservation Area**

Through a veil of egrets a bull elephant gazes across the Ngorongoro Crater's grassy floor, the forested crater wall behind him. One of the world's geological wonders, Ngorongoro sustains a wealth of wildlife inside a lushly vegetated volcanic caldera over ten miles wide, with a circular rampart 2,000 feet high. Beyond the crater the conservation area extends to the border of the Serengeti National Park, and some animals migrate between park and crater. Unlike the park, the conservation area is open to Masai herders. Their traditional practice of continually moving their cattle was ecologically sound: It prevented overgrazing the savanna. Now, however, there are more Masai, and they roam less— and so the common African problem of overgrazing has come to parts of the conservation area. But not to the crater itself; cattle can come in here wildlife. The poachers were the army, security officers, and government officials who provided illegal hunters with automatic weapons. From 1973 to 1980 elephant populations in Murchison Falls National Park declined from 14,300 to 2,000, and in Queen Elizabeth National Park, from 2,700 to 700. Then came the war of liberation, and as armies contended across the country, wildlife was ruined again.

In the past decade, poachers have killed almost all the 4,000 black rhinos and 100,000 elephants of the wildlife sanctuaries of Zambia. Their own game decimated, Zambian poachers are crossing the Zambezi River into Zimbabwe. Since 1984, when the poachers began their raids, they have killed more than 200 rhinos in the Zambezi Valley. The hunters are often met by antipoaching squads, and more than 30 poachers have died in firefights. Even in Kenya, the center of African environmentalism, all is not well. Poachers have reduced elephant populations by two-thirds in Tsavo East and Tsavo West National Parks. And one recent November night a gang of heavily armed poachers opened fire on rangers' quarters in Meru National Park. The invaders gunned down rhinos, cut off their horns, and vanished into the bush.

There are happier stories. In 1980 Malawi established Lake Malawi National Park, the first deepwater lake reserve in Africa. That lake's 400 fish species live nowhere else on earth. Niger's Aïr and Ténéré National Nature Reserve protects remnant antelope populations of addaxes and oryx. Amboseli Game Reserve in southern Kenya has been innovative in its attempts to bring local landowners—the Masai—into the economy of the reserve. The Masai Mara National Reserve of Kenya, at the border with Tanzania and the Serengeti, accommodates the northern migrations of the last great herds of African wildlife. These and the other parks of Africa must succeed, or we, the generation now alive, really will have seen the last of the game.

Tanzania

Kilimanjaro National Park

Somewhere up here, on the rim of the ancient volcano's crater, early rays of dawn are warming another party of tired, chilled hikers. Every year hundreds of tourists brave arctic cold, equatorial sun, and thin air to attempt the five-day trek up Kilimanjaro and back. They see changing zones of life on the way. On lower slopes of the mountain, which covers an area as big as Rhode Island, the industrious Chagga tribe maintains small farmsteads, or shambas, watered by irrigation canals that trap runoff from above. From the park boundary at 6,000 feet to 9,500 feet, a cloud forest drips moisture. Above the periodic cloud deck the forest opens into heather, which shades into moorland, and then at 14,500 feet, to alpine desert. The hikers' final push begins at 1 a.m. on the fourth day, over gravel, rock, and snow to greet the morning sun atop the crater rim, 19,340 feet high—the crown of Africa.

Tanzania

Serengeti National Park

In a dark rumble of mud and hoof, wildebeests spill down the bank of a river during their migration across the Serengeti. The park protects about half of this grassland ecosystem. It feeds over two million plains mammals—the largest such congregation on earth. Most of them—wildebeests, gazelles, and zebras—follow a 500-mile clockwise migration route: from southeastern plains to western woodlands, then north to Kenya's Masai Mara, and finally south again as rains return to the southeastern plains. When the wet season ends, zebras generally take the lead, cropping the high grass. The massive wildebeest herd follows, eating medium-high growth. Gazelles can then get at the exposed short grasses. The rotating migration pattern maximizes the number of grazers the land can support, a method now copied by a few American cattle ranchers.

Namibia

Namib-Naukluft Park

Well adapted to desert life, a gemsbok walks the sand sea of the Namib Desert, where no rain may fall for years. When necessary this African oryx can survive without drinking, taking its moisture from vegetation. Sharp, long horns protect against predators.

The huge dunes lie between the 6,000-foot-high Naukluft Mountains and the southwest African coast. These dry sandpiles owe their existence to floodwater. Rivers south of here deposited sediment where winds or ocean currents could carry it to the Namib. Stiff South Atlantic breezes whip it into dunes up to a thousand feet high. The same onshore winds support a rainless ecosystem; even after drought has sent the gemsbok to slightly greener pastures, the fog that blows in over the dunes every few days supplies enough moisture to sustain a host of beetles, spiders, and snakes.

Masai Mara National Reserve

Ears on full alert, impalas seek the source of a clicking shutter on the grassland of the Masai Mara, the northern tip of the Serengeti ecosystem. Unlike some other antelope, the impalas do not need to migrate in search of grass; breeding herds like this one can graze or browse a variety of vegetation, enabling them to wander about within the same region regardless of season.

The Mara reserve exists by consent of the Masai tribe, whose lands it occupies. But during droughts, the Masai may let their cattle encroach on the reserve, endangering wildlife food supplies. Perhaps less environmentally threatening, but more annoying, are the scores of tourist vans that prowl the Mara; tourism to Kenya has surpassed half a million visitors a year.

Frans Lanting

Zaïre

Virunga National Park

A mountain stream gurgles beneath stalks of giant lobelias (on left) high in the Ruwenzori, Ptolemy's "Mountains of the Moon," located at the north end of the Virunga National Park. The Ruwenzori's unusual vegetation bolsters Virunga's claim to encompassing the greatest variety of habitats of any park in Africa.

The park extends south to include the Virunga mountain range, whose few volcanic peaks rise on the frontiers of three nations. The park in Zaïre, the adjoining Volcanoes National Park in Rwanda, and the Kigezi sanctuary in Uganda constitute the last stronghold of the mountain gorilla, the endangered great ape brought to fame by the studies of Dian Fossey in Rwanda. Two volcanoes in the Virunga park, Nyiragongo and Nyamlagira, erupt every few years, fueled by a slow rifting in earth's crust.

Algeria

Tassili-n-Ajjer National Park

A forest of dry rock stands where once the sweet water ran—about 8,000 years ago in Tassili. At a time when Ice Age glaciers entombed much of Europe, this plateau in the heart of the Sahara blossomed under balmy rains, which helped carve the sandstone towers. The water nurtured an unknown people, the first of many to leave paintings and engravings on Tassili's canyon walls. These pictures—thousands of them now—tell a long story: of Neolithic hunters, shown stalking now extinct buffalo; of pastoralists who appeared around 4000 B.C., using sticks to herd cattle; and of Tuareg nomads, who began coming here with their camels after the glaciers had melted and the rains moved a thousand miles north. Still, the Tuareg knew or remembered the past, for it was they who named this realm of sun and dust Tassili-n-Ajjer—"plateau of the rivers."

79

Giraffes stand against twilight in Botswana's Chobe National Park, a bright oasis of preservation on a continent where much wilderness faces its last sundown.

Life on the Edge of Thirst

They call it *pula* in the Setswana language. It is so important here that they made it the nation's one-word motto, emblazoned under Botswana's national shield: PULA. Its worth is so great they named the currency for it—a pula for a Coke, a few hundred pula for a good cow. They put pale blue stripes on the flag to represent it. At weddings well-wishers cry "pula!" to the newlyweds. It is fundamental to the politics of diamonds and beef and lions: pula.

Rain.

Over the roar of wind and engine I shout a tourist's question forward to Tim Liversedge, our pilot and consulting naturalist. "Why are so many of the pans round?" A pan is any shallow depression that holds rainwater, no matter its size. On the savanna below, a scattering of small pans glints up at us. It is March, and they brim with the summer's accumulation of rain. The seven-year drought has finally ended.

Air is blasting into the Cessna's cabin; we had removed the door so Frans Lanting could aim his cameras at the flat landscape unimpeded. Tim yells an answer back, but I can't hear it. From the rear seat I watch the green, tree-sprinkled savanna of Chobe National Park go by under Frans's elbow. Among the trees, we have seen antelope, giraffes, wildebeests, and a disproportionate number of zebras. That's good; the autumn zebra migration will be peaking when we return to this area—the Savute Marsh—by Land-Rover. We turn west to follow the Savute Channel, leaving Chobe behind. Although mysteriously dry for several years now, the channel grows sufficiently deep farther "upstream" for water to pool in low parts. At the center of each pool, a cluster of hippopotamus backs gleams darkly.

We bank again, heading back south, and pass over drier country. Here we see little of the game common near the pans and pools.

National Parks and Reserves of Northern Botswana

Chobe & Nxai Pan National Parks

At the fringes of the Kalahari Desert—the Land of Thirst—the wildlife of northern Botswana relies on annual rains and on subsequent flooding of the Kwando and Okavango Rivers. The Okavango forms a great inland delta, spreading out on

Moremi Wildlife Reserve

top of sediments trapped by a shallow branch of Africa's Great Rift Valley. Bracketing the delta, faults outline the buried sides of the rift. A little of the Okavango's annual floodwater reaches the Boteti River, which trickles to its death in the

Makgadikgadi Pans Game Reserve

flat, wide basin of the Makgadikgadi salt pans. Southwestward lies the Kalahari, more an arid savanna than a true desert. Here new boreholes will provide water for game, which has been cut off from northern rivers by livestock fences.

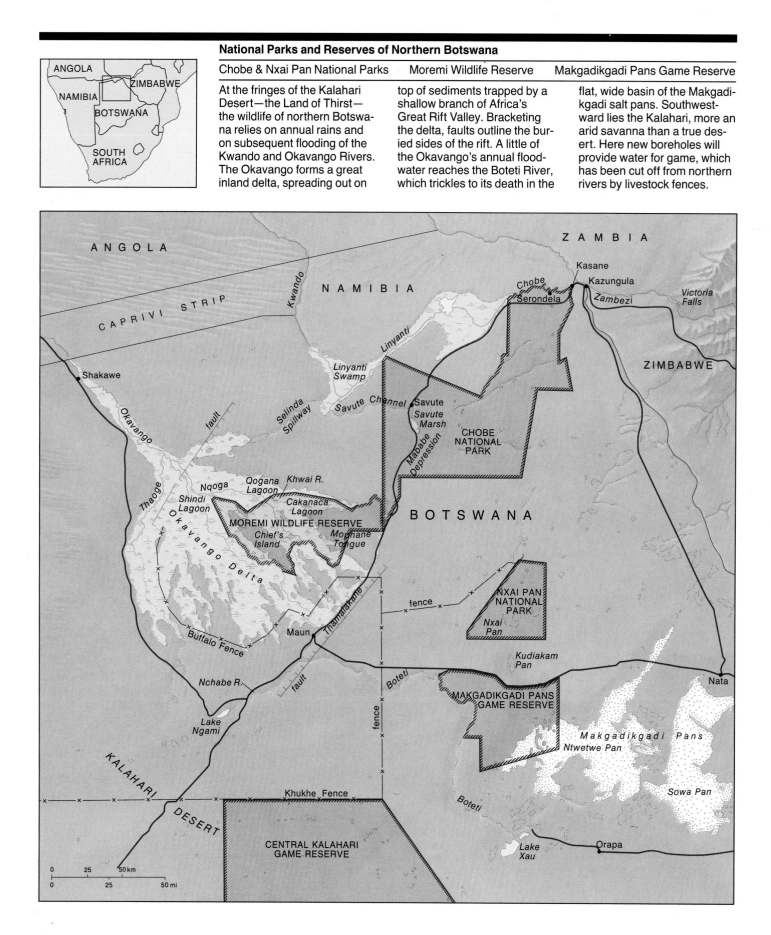

Traces of ancient watercourses, dry for ages, etch the terrain. A silent warning.

Abruptly the land turns lushly green. We have reached the Moremi Wildlife Reserve, part of an immense inland delta—an immense oasis, some say of it. It is the not-quite-final resting-place of one of southern Africa's mightiest rivers, the Okavango.

A fish eagle soars by just below us; an elephant, alone and so probably an old bull, wades in a marsh lavishly flooded with rain.

Rainwater comes twice a year to semiarid northern Botswana—but only once from the sky. The showers that are just ending peaked in January and February—Southern Hemisphere summer. They settle the dust of the long, dry winter and the hotter, drier spring. Wildlife spreads out into newly green countryside, and overgrazed, trampled land around riverbanks gets a chance to recover. For a few months the pans will serve the hordes of the thirsty. That's what Tim was trying to tell me: A small pan gets beaten into a circular shape by the legions of hooves and paws that converge on it, and by the overheated bodies that.wallow in it.

This yearly cycle of rain and drought typifies a savanna, the open mix of grassland and trees prevalent in Botswana. More rain, and you would get forest or marsh, like the one below us; less, a desert, like the deep Kalahari southwest of here. In sparsely peopled Botswana, the mix tilts toward desert.

A few minutes after leaving Moremi, we

Trees, sedges, and reeds thrive on the watery floodplain of the Okavango Delta. Most of the Okavango's flow vanishes in such marshes, sucked into the dry air either by evaporation or indirectly by transpiration—by way of the leaves and grasses. Hippos probably left the trails in the grass; in time they may become new channels.

A dazzle of zebras drinks at a Chobe pan during their April migration, when the animals mass in the Savute Marsh, seeking fresh, tall grasses. The grass will grow back after the zebras disperse—a respite denied overstocked areas outside the parks. There sedentary goats and cattle often denude rangeland, especially near water.

fly across the Buffalo Fence, perhaps the most important of Botswana's controversial cattle fences. The ruler-straight line of post and wire transects the flatness. Southward, brush fences begin to appear. Several cattle graze next to one of them, on ground already brown and nearly barren. On the other side of the fence the land is green.

To get through the year, life in these parts depends on the region's second influx of rainwater. It will arrive by land: the annual flood of the Okavango, fed by rains over the river's watershed in distant Angola. The flood crest will have seeped through the delta just when the dry season is at its height. As the pans turn to dust, wild game migrates scores of miles to the newly flowing channels. The much cherished cattle will also water there. All of northern Botswana responds to the pulse of the Okavango flood.

And so do the politics of nature. The region's parks and reserves—Chobe, Moremi, Nxai Pan, and Makgadikgadi Pans—protect some of the best, least abused wilderness in Africa. Botswana has set aside fully 17 percent of its territory for wildlife. Though severely short of trained staff for the parks, the government has been making an effort —an exceptional effort by African standards—to defend the parks and reserves against cattle incursions and poaching. Still, the borders drawn to protect wildlife must also accommodate the water needs of people and livestock. Park and reserve borders cannot therefore encompass all of the huge ecosystem they are meant to preserve.

We land back at the town of Maun, a thriving sprawl of commercial buildings, mud huts, and comfortable thatched villas. Maun is the main safari base for the region. The drive from the airport reveals a population mix unusually diverse for Botswana. The country owes its stable democratic government in part to having only one major ethnic group, the Batswana (the singular is Motswana). But along this road you also see Herero women, swaddled in colorful

An impala doe takes a morning cud-chewing break in Chobe. Her herd watches for danger. If the antelope feel threatened, they may scatter in an explosion of graceful leaps as much as 10 feet high and 30 feet long.

Victorian-style dresses; an international mix of whites charging around in four-wheel-drive vehicles; and the occasional San (Bushman) bringing in some handicrafts to sell at a curio store.

Tourism may be booming, but it is cattle that make a Motswana's heart sing—and a wildlife preservationist's sink.

"Our livelihood is purely cattle," says K. S. Bingana, who holds a highly respected position: manager of the Meat Commission in Maun. He tells me that the Batswana regard their cattle as Americans do their savings accounts. And wealth confers status: "If the man who has more cattle than others speaks, people tend to listen to him."

But cattle need more water than native antelope, tear up grass by the roots, and trample the earth into hard-packed wasteland, particularly around water holes. In a drought, they leave little to regenerate. Then both cattle and wildlife starve.

Such vying for food and water increasing-ly threatens Africa's wild animals and the parks that protect them. Although people on distant continents speak of "lions in the jungles of Africa," most of Africa is not jungle, but desert or savanna. Most of Africa's great wild mammals live in the savanna. So do numerous cattle and goats. Africa has the fastest growing human population in the world, and many of these people like owning cattle. The problems deepen with drought, and drought is common. The land turns to dust then, even in cattle-free parks.

"Last November, it looked so bad here that people said Savute was dead, that it would never recover. Dust blew everywhere. Everything looked gray from the sky to the ground," says Brodie Calef. I had arrived the day before, here in Chobe National Park, crown jewel of Botswana's wildlife areas, and now ride in the back of the jouncing pickup driven by George, Brodie's biologist husband. We gaze out on one of the park's main attractions. Frans and I had seen it from the air just a few days ago: the lush, tall grass of the Savute Marsh—although a marsh it has not been for years.

Out in that grass, making a dry swishing as they move, are zebras—thousands of them. The migration is in full swing—not thundering herds, like the wildebeests of Tanzania's Serengeti, but a casual amassing of individual families. Zebras graze in the tall grass and hover nervously around the pans. One group gallops onto the track in front of us, then veers off into the *mophane* scrub that surrounds the marsh.

No one knows for sure why the zebras gather at Savute, or even exactly where they come from. Mark Vandewalle, a graduate student here doing his thesis on grazing patterns, thinks that nutrients from the channel have enriched the soil, and that the correspondingly good grazing attracts zebras when the pans hold water to drink.

The channel stopped flowing in 1981. We don't know why, though there are theories: drought, earthquake, or papyrus blockages upstream. History notes earlier stoppages; the flow may resume. But I think of the fossil watercourses I saw from the plane.

George and Brodie Calef live next to the grassy channel, in one of the tents at the Chobe Lion Research Camp. Frans and I share the tent next door. George, a bearded Canadian, used to study caribou in the Yukon and now studies elephants for the Botswana government, tracking them with radio collars and looking into the sensitive question of whether Botswana needs a culling program. He and Brodie also contend with the vervet monkeys that run around camp pinching things, the spotted hyenas that keep breaking into the deep freeze at night, and a big elephant named Baby Huey that has developed a taste for fruit and a willingness to destroy any closed vehicle keeping him from it. Huey is now considered dangerous and "incredibly destructive," but has not been seen in months.

It is Easter weekend, height of the tourist influx from South Africa, and about as crowded as Savute ever gets, which isn't very. But this is Easter and someone has spotted lions: a pride dozing next to a pan. You can drive right up to them. Brodie and I count 41 people in 7 vehicles watching 5 lions sleep. Almost half the watchers sit on the roof of one pickup camper: a school class up from Pietermaritzburg. It is a good thing attacks on vehicles are rare; the teenagers' bare legs hang over the sides like a row of lion Popsicles.

In Botswana this fascination with wildlife still seems a preoccupation primarily of whites. Botswana started the parks and runs them, but the aesthetics of nature are not uppermost on the mind of the average rural citizen of a developing nation.

Bingana had told me how country people were commonly raised to deal with wildlife. "Anything that you see, you kill. You people, when you see a beautiful little bird, you will stand and appreciate it, and say, 'Isn't that pretty?' Now when we see something like that, we collect a stone, and throw it, and say 'Kill it!' " He laughed: such a contrast. For a people steeped in pastoralism, wildlife is subsistence food, or dangerous vermin, or just not relevant. Hardly a surprise: Think of settlers' attitudes in the American West. Think of cattlemen battling environmentalists there today.

In Botswana things are changing. Some educated urban blacks now visit the parks as tourists. Conservationists both black and white campaign to educate the public about wildlife. The expanding Wildlife Training Centre in Maun is preparing an intensive new training program for government wildlife employees. "Everyone in the Wildlife Department will go through that program," vows a senior game warden.

For now it is the multinational community of whites, by and large, who take people into the parks and who study and film and write about wildlife. A few were born in Botswana, but the rest are either non-African or descendants of the British Empire—African-born British who migrated here from Zimbabwe, Zambia, or East Africa.

We head back late in the day. Ranks of puffy, flat-bottomed cumulus recede across an unceasing sky. Far out on the open plain, two lone gray bumps graze—bull elephants, like reapers at the end of time.

Elephants exude that sense of agelessness. They are large, intelligent, sociable, long lived, deliberate, dusty, and wrinkled. They appear older than we. Wiser. I remember seeing a film of an elephant-culling operation in Rwanda. The procedure is to shoot an entire family, except babies, so that survivors won't panic the rest of the herd. The shock was not just that the great beings could be dropped so fast, by such small things as bullets, but that it seemed the very hills were falling.

At dusk the next day we sit with Mark in Land-Rovers next to a pan. We are waiting. In front of us half a dozen lions have been entertainingly napping all day. We are waiting for them to wake up, in hopes of observing the hunt. Mark has agreed to help us.

The sun sets, washing the sky red. We eat supper from thermos bottles. Darkness deepens, Venus shines brightly, and the lions sleep on. A metallic *clink-clink-clink* sounds as a blacksmith plover flies over. The Milky Way arches across the sky. Finally the lions stretch and rise. They move off, hunger on their minds.

Mark starts his engine and we follow, shadowing them noisily. Now the big cats look anything but lazy. Briefly caught in Mark's headlights, the pride moves low, swift, and purposeful, not walking so much as rippling through the grass.

Our pursuit comes to a sudden halt when an ant-bear burrow gives way beneath a front wheel. Our Land-Rover must be laboriously jacked and winched out. With lions on the prowl it pays to be cautious, so we take turns aiming a spotlight into the night. In the middle distance an arc of eyes glints

brightly in the beam: hyenas, monitoring our operation with interest.

Half an hour later we have extricated ourselves and resume cautiously cruising through the night. Somewhere—where?—a lion calls to the pride: a low, quiet purr-growl, almost subsonic. In the deep shadow under a tree, a small sea of alert impala eyes glimmers greenly in the headlights. Finally, at moonrise, we give up and return to camp, to hear that our lions did kill a zebra, only to be chased off by hyenas. The two carnivores often steal each other's kills.

The evening leaves me impressed with the African night—the desperate *importance* of the night. With every sundown, some new, deadly drama begins, its outcome to be revealed by light of dawn in a lioness's still-gaunt rib cage, or in the skittish dance of tired zebras unnerved by dark moments of fright and flight.

At about 3 a.m. an additional bit of drama awakens me: a persistent clanking outside our tent. Hyenas trying to get into our Land-Rover? All I can see through the open tent flap is a pale gray patch of moonlit sky. The clanking goes on. I slip out of bed and peer outside, to discover the gray patch isn't sky; it is the side of a huge bull elephant. *Huey.* His trunk is working at the hatch of the Land-Rover. Inside are all Frans's cameras and—of course!—our food box.

Not sure what a naked man should do when confronting a large, "incredibly destructive" elephant, I do what any other man would. I put on my pants. Luckily Mark has heard the ruckus by this time and shows up yelling and waving a flashlight. Huey backs off. So that's what you do.

At 6 a.m. Huey tries again. I shout and he drifts away to surveillance range and dawdles there, tearing off bunches of grass and looking innocent. George soon shows up, grinning: "So Huey tried to eat your Land-Rover, eh?" He goes back to his camp and reappears in his truck. Beeping the horn, he begins herding the elephant with the little

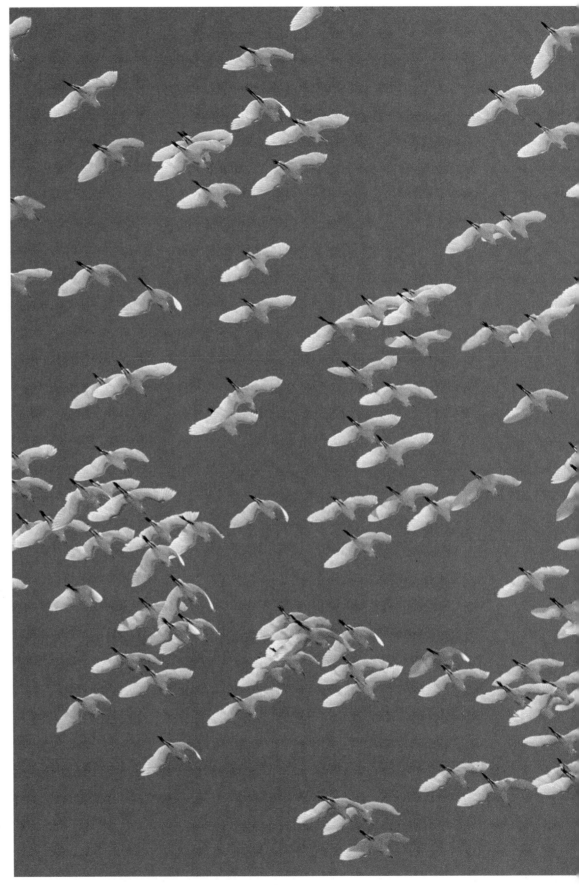

Cattle egrets fill the sky over Chobe. A larger cousin, the great white egret (above), stalks its prey—a fish or frog, most likely—in the shallows of the Chobe River. At Savute a yellow-billed hornbill (upper) holds a wiggly meal. In dry lands, food alone can provide enough moisture to keep a hornbill going.

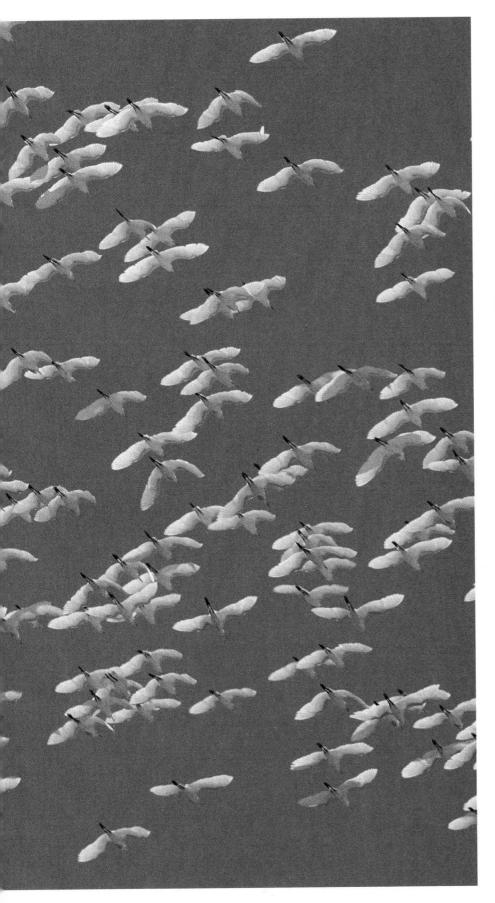

white pickup. Huey retreats massively toward the dry channel. As the sky lightens, Huey, the beeping, and the taillights of his tormentor dwindle into the bush.

Huey's story is not that funny, though. During the drought a safari camp operator had begun feeding him—an easy error in African parks. Once accustomed to people such "habituated" elephants overstep the bounds of politeness, and safety. Then, if every measure fails, they must be shot.

And two months later, Huey was.

It is autumn in Chobe, and you can see winter coming—the rainless time. Winter has already crept into the dry soil between the green blades of tall grass. It hovers in the dust trails a Land Cruiser throws up even after one of the season's last, brief showers. The zebras have moved on, almost all of them. We move on as well, to Chobe's other main attraction, its river.

The Chobe River links the Linyanti Swamp, a miniature version of the Okavango Delta, to the Zambezi River. Seen from the high banks of the Serondela camping area, the Chobe is a beautiful, gently winding river, sparkling under a blue sky and begging to be swum in—probably not a good idea for people, given the hippos, crocodiles, and bilharzias lurking in the cheery wavelets. It's fine, though, for elephants.

"In the dry season you can sometimes see hundreds along the riverbank," says the guide we retained. You could also see them being, well, incredibly destructive: During the drought, they broke trees, pushed trees down, and ringbarked trees, which then died standing. They devastated much of the forest near the river—or so it seems.

It is a problem George works on, an unusual one: Are there too many elephants? In countries north of here elephant populations are plunging, their habitat whittled away by farmland, their numbers slashed by ivory poachers. But in Botswana they are multiplying as fast as biology allows.

Scientists differ on the seriousness of

the problem, even whether it is a problem. Often an elephant-felled tree remains attached at the roots, and the branches survive, providing shelter for small animals and protecting plants underneath from trampling. It might even be that forests are unnaturally thick because overhunting in the 1800s had killed too many elephants.

But a new forest takes decades to grow, and elephants need other places to live in the meantime. That kind of time and space is growing scarce in modern Africa. So George has few choices to consider: 1. Do nothing and hope the ecosystem can adjust. 2. Lift some or all of Botswana's six-year ban on elephant hunting and risk driving still more elephants into the parks. 3. Cull.

Morning on the open Chobe floodplain. A greater kudu bull, bearing a splendor of spiraled horns, leads three cows through the tall grass. A troop of baboons fools around nearby, keeping several lookouts posted, each atop a termite hill. Not until dusk, though, do we see gray shapes filing silently across the dusty main road, heading for the river. From a low bluff we watch as the elephants drink and bathe in water aglow with sunset. Shoulder deep, two bulls spar in leisurely fashion, splashing copper. They trundle to the bank as a tourist boat chugs past—the evening "booze cruise" from Chobe Game Lodge. The Holocene displacing the Pleistocene.

Yet without tourism's economic benefits

Drowsing at dawn by a pan, young lions may continue to sleep all day, until time to tank up for the evening hunt. "Contagious activity," as one researcher calls it, typifies lions: One drinks, all drink.

NEXT PAGES: Refreshed from watering and spraying themselves at a pan, elephants head into the Chobe bush to feed. A national hunting ban and a low rate of poaching have left Botswana's elephants willing to tolerate close approaches by people.

A hyena specialist at Savute tracks her subjects with an antenna tuned to radio collars that she put on the animals after tranquilizing them. Chewing on an elephant carcass (lower left), a hyena upholds its scavenger image, but researchers now know hyenas often hunt their own prey, like these (upper) drinking after a zebra kill.

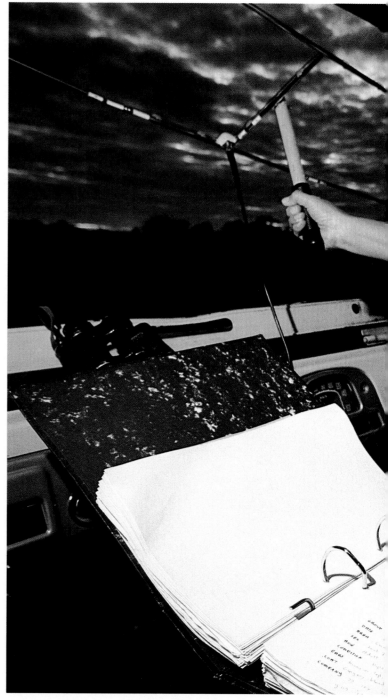

Africa's national parks could disappear. By citing tourism, conservationists can persuade a cattle-minded country that wildlife is worth keeping.

They cite trophy hunting, too. Some of Africa's last "great white hunters" work in Botswana, leading safaris. Overseas clients, many from America, may pay $16,000 for a three-week safari, plus license and trophy fees—it costs $2,000 to bag a lion, for instance—and expenses such as taxidermy.

After we leave Chobe and return to Maun, we visit the sizable taxidermy shop that Ken Oakes runs outside town, next to a menagerie he operates for wildlife film projects. He and his chief taxidermist appear content to celebrate nature by both filming it and stuffing it. The two men take us around the menagerie, showing us jackals, bat-eared foxes, springhares, and ant bears—what Americans know as aardvarks. One cage houses a small hawk, and the taxidermist pauses to make cooing noises.

We walk back toward the shop. "Do you want a snarl on that lion, Ken?" asks the taxidermist. Back to work. Scattered about the open-walled shop are animals in varying stages of reconstruction. In one corner an entire lion stands on its mount. I stroke the tawny back. The thought comes unbidden: "Wish you were still in the bush, don't you, boy?" I understand, of course, that trophy hunting appears actually to be helping the wildlife, since enormous tracts outside the parks are designated "controlled hunting areas," free of overexploitation. I know that quotas are reset every year to keep game populations healthy. I understand that for people with Hemingway in their blood, "to shoot a wild lion in Africa" is a dream worth the fortune they willingly pay. But as the rough hair passes beneath my fingers, I myself must still struggle to understand why.

So it was ironic and instructive for me to have witnessed a meeting where hunters asked to continue a hunting ban that an environmentalist was thinking of lifting.

The rubber-necked ogle the long-necked in Chobe, where many animals have grown accustomed to tourists on game drives. The giraffes' height gives them a browsing monopoly on upper branches—of *mophane* (MO-PA-nay) trees here.

Two professional hunters had flown to Savute to lobby George about elephants. They wanted elephant trophy hunting legalized as a business, yes—but not if it meant open hunting for the general public. "Botswana is one of the only countries in Africa where elephant are not being poached to any great extent," one of them told me. "We felt that if legal public hunting were allowed, it would give rise to illegal hunting, and poaching would run riot. Elsewhere elephant poaching is just rife—everywhere, absolutely everywhere."

He had worked in the parks of Zambia's Luangwa Valley, watching 80 percent of its elephants vanish in only a few years. Poachers used automatic rifles. "It was like a war going on. Every day you heard shots from poachers, and sometimes hundreds of shots." He adjusted his broad-brimmed white-hunter hat. "We're dead against even ourselves being allowed to shoot elephant again. The few that are available should be top quality, and they should be offered to overseas clients, and all the income should be distributed among the locals."

That, too, is conservationist strategy: Be sure local people get the benefits and maybe they won't vote to open the reserves to cattle. Appeal to economics, not aesthetics.

Landlocked and seemingly resource-poor, the protectorate the British had called Bechuanaland became the independent nation of Botswana in 1966. Almost the size of Texas, but with fewer people than San Antonio, it was born one of the world's poorest countries, a black-ruled land economically dependent on the nemesis next door—white-ruled South Africa. Yet today Botswana is relatively prosperous, thanks to newfound diamond deposits and to beef exports. Neither comes without cost.

The European Community, which subsidizes the beef industry, requires that Botswana control foot-and-mouth disease. The easiest way is to section rangeland with long fences to contain outbreaks. But the

fences also contain wildlife, blocking little-understood migration routes. In the early 1980s, drought sent tens of thousands of wildebeests in the huge Central Kalahari Game Reserve north, heading for the rivers. They found instead the Khukhe Fence. Many died there. They may have died anyway; droughts cause die-offs even at rivers, mainly by starvation. But this toll, perhaps 90 percent of Kalahari wildebeests, sparked an international outcry that has led planners to route future fences with more care.

The Buffalo Fence was another matter— a deft bit of political judo. By law, the Okavango Delta was cattle free, but law is a fragile barrier. Trading on findings that wild buffalo carry foot-and-mouth, conservationists promoted a fence to protect cattle by keeping buffalo in their main habitat— the delta. Coincidentally, the fence also keeps cattle *out* of the delta and its Moremi Wildlife Reserve. Just in time, say some.

Until now at least, the primary engineers

Jaw to jaw and maw to maw, hippopotamuses argue a point in the Chobe River. Many of the testy animals bear scars from bites by their peers.

Clouds over the Okavango Delta reflect from Qogana Lagoon. Unlike the seasonally dry outer delta, Qogana is "perennial" water; the Okavango keeps the lagoon filled year-round.

of this ever changing system of marshes, channels, and islands have been papyrus, hippos, termites, and the living earth itself. After the Okavango flows across Botswana's border and meanders through a flood-plain called the Panhandle, it fans out into a hand shape a hundred miles long. Seen from space the delta makes such a striking contrast with the surrounding semidesert that U. S. astronaut Walter Schirra paid a visit after one flight to satisfy his curiosity.

We choose a lower altitude than Wally's, flying over tree-covered islands surrounded by flooded fields of papyrus. These papyrus beds can gradually thicken into dams that reroute channels. Earth tremors may also affect channels; the entire delta overlies a buried branch of Africa's tectonically active rift valley system, and tremors may retilt the flat terrain just enough to redirect water flow. Here and there narrow lines of open water cut through the vegetation: channels kept open mainly by hippos, the dredges of the Okavango.

Below us a tiny island, consisting of a single tree and a tall termite mound, bespeaks the termites' contribution. Their hills help start small islands. Silting may build larger islands. The largest of all, 40-mile-long Chief's Island, lies within the Moremi Wild-life Reserve. Both island and reserve are named for the ruling family of the local Batawana tribe, which agreed in 1963 to set aside these lands for wildlife.

Our pilot leaves us at an airstrip just north of Moremi. We wait. There are no tsetse flies to slap; almost all are gone, eradicated by government spraying. It was the disease-carrying flies that kept cattle out of the delta. Now only law and Buffalo Fence stand against the bovine multitude.

A boatman arrives and taxis us to Shindi safari camp, through scenery a world away from the dust of Chobe. The narrow channels twist confusingly through a water-logged forest of papyrus. The feathery umbels of their heads bow just overhead. In

Tranquil water lilies in a delta lagoon provide good hunting for creatures of the Moremi reserve. A jacana (above), its long toes splayed for support on lily pads, seeks insects. A reed frog needs seek no further. Reed frogs vary so much in coloring they have been called snowflakes of the frog world—no two alike.

still narrower channels you have to duck down to the gunwales to get through. Now and then we pop out into an open lagoon, zoom across it and into another almost invisible channel on the far side. A person could get lost in a place like this.

The channels are narrow, but the riverway isn't; shallow water may spread through the papyrus beds for miles. Everywhere, even in the lagoons, a current is detectable. Filtered by the papyrus, the clear water is so pure that it's said you can drink it right from the boat. This marsh flows.

We overnight at Shindi camp, managed by Daryl Balfour, a genially morose South African journalist who says he's working here while he does his book on "the rape of the Okavango." With Daryl's three Australian clients we swap yarns around the campfire over after-dinner coffee, a treasured safari camp ritual. Daryl tells about the time the lion roared back at the guy who snored so loud, from right outside his tent.

They're not just tourist entertainment, these animal stories. You hear them everywhere, in the camps, at parties, in bars, waiting for planes. Some stories are funny or weird; some are not. The time the drought got so bad the lions drank every night from the big birdbath at Lloyd's Camp. The hyena at the Savute airstrip that developed a taste for airplane tails and would cause thousands of pula in damage with one munch. That ostrich down at Oudtshoorn that was a hundred years old and still laying. The female pet mongoose that so hated other females, of any species, that when women clients arrived in camp, she would scurry up their clothes and nip them on the lip. The time a black mamba, or maybe it was a cobra, bit Bobby Wilmot; how he struggled back to his camp and tried to inject himself with the only antivenin he had, except it spilled. And how he then spent the last hours of his life writing farewell letters to his wife and family.

If you drift downstream from Shindi,

you'll come eventually to Cakanaca Lagoon, where the water lilies stretch on for miles and where African jacanas, or lily-trotters, mince their way from pad to pad in search of insects, untroubled by a life spent on footing that is forever giving way beneath them. At day's end we float here, watching and listening. A fish eagle and mate call to each other. Reed cormorants, night herons, and white-faced tree ducks come and go. Sundown . . . twilight . . . and as darkness falls white and blue water lilies close their blossoms; yellow ones open. A full moon shines —two of them really, one in the sky and one floating among the lotus petals, reflected so clearly you can see the Sea of Rains.

Next day, we go by Land-Rover into the dry peninsula called the Mophane Tongue —mainland Moremi. We lunch by a hippo pool, and three sets of eyes, ears, and nostrils drift over to watch. Since hippos can't take the sun, they graze at night and stay immersed by day: half asleep at times, sluggishly restless at others; wetly, whooshily exhaling; twirling their tiny ears; trying to bite each other; yawning their huge pink yawns; and defecating in each other's faces —said to be a sign of submission, yet. Every now and then one will emit a stentorian HRNGHK-HRNGHK-HRNGHK through its jumbo nostrils. After one hippo HRNGHKS, the whole lot may take it up for a minute or so—"like old men cawing over a dirty joke," the guides say. They are loud, nasty, fat, and gross—a caricature of everything we hold repellent. They are wonderful.

In a couple of months or so the level in the hippo pools will rise as the flood crest moves through. Slowly the water will overflow into the dry outer delta. The earth will soak it up. So will the grass and trees. So will the air— two inches of water a week. The frogs that mated when the rains came will mate again.

People wonder: Will there be a good flood this year? No one knows. There is civil war in Angola, and no weather reports.

Even if the flood is good, less than five

percent will percolate all the way through the delta. Diverted by a low uplift along a fault—the southeastern side of the buried rift valley—some of this surviving water will coalesce into the Thamalakane River, and some will leak over the low lip of the rift into the Boteti.

When it flows, the Boteti drains toward the great, shallow basin of the Makgadikgadi, where the flat, salt-encrusted expanse of the million-year-old lake bed lies dry as chalk much of the year, and where the powdery dust storms can bear down on you, they say, "like a moving mountain range." The Boteti no longer reaches the pans, but it is still the longest, last gasp of the Okavango system, and many animals

of Nxai Pan National Park and the Makgadikgadi Pans Game Reserve depend on it.

In predawn darkness we jounce along an overgrown back road to Nxai Pan. (The "x" is a click in one of the San languages.) Thornbush scrapes the side of the Land-Rover, and from time to time the headlights pick up a huge orb spiderweb strung across the track. At dawn we pause near Kudiakam Pan, by Baines's Baobabs, painted by artist Thomas Baines in 1862. Some tourists have camped under the squat, bulbously dramatic trees, just as Livingstone did when he journeyed through here in the 1850s. The sun is well up when we pass an old Shell service station sign, painted over with a stenciled "WELL COME TO NXAI PAN."

A fish eagle in Moremi displays its prowess. More patient if less flashy, a crocodile awaits a meal—bird, fish, or a land animal careless enough to get too near. Two farms in Botswana are trying to raise crocs for meat and hides, in hopes of demonstrating the reptile's value as a national resource.

National parks have limited budgets.

Nxai Pan is a wide fossil pan that apparently had an outlet once; whatever water used to drain through here left rich sediments rather than the salt and soda evaporites of the Makgadikgadi. The resulting fertile, grassy savanna attracts animals much as Savute Marsh does. Springbok, zebras, and wildebeests graze under the noonday sun. Anywhere near them, or us, flies buzz—the sound of daylight in Africa.

As the dry season worsens, many of these animals will drift southward to meet the remnants of the Okavango flood as it trickles down the Boteti. Conservationists hope to extend a corridor south from the park to the Makgadikgadi reserve, which protects river access, and so secure this entire migration route, as well as Baines's Baobabs.

We drift south, too, into the wide open reaches of the reserve. A nearby thundercloud darkens half the sky. Crosslighted in the westering sun, the grasslands become fields of waving silver under purple velvet.

And there we find gemsbok, the dashing southern African oryx—a herd of 35 or so (a dozen is normal)—prancing, tail-swishing, with a forest of long rapier horns above gray coats in bold black-and-white trim. They string out in single file across the plain, making for one startling moment a scene of Euclidean beauty, all straight lines: flat horizon, file of antelope, horns angled high, a sunbeam slanting down from the clouds.

Like giant lily pads, islands of grass stand out from the sea of dried mud forming the fringe of the Makgadikgadi Pans. The name means roughly "place of huge drying up." The pans—dusty, salty, ironing-board flat, nearly lifeless—extend for scores of miles. Only after rains cover them with a thin sheet of water does life flourish there—spectacularly. Flamingos then find conditions for raising their young are ideal: shallow water, far from predators on shore. The birds feed on algae and on tiny brine shrimp whose eggs can survive years of drought and hatch whenever enough water collects.

We camp near here on a low rise under a few lonely trees, and cook supper while lightning flickers far out over the plain.

Across that plain, the Boteti awaits the flood. On the north shore, the new water will sustain wildlife; on the south, cattle; and downriver—the Orapa diamond mine. The mine reservoir will take whatever it can. Diamonds have brought income to a land that needed it badly. But processing the ore takes enormous amounts of water, and the Boteti doesn't supply enough.

Orapa needs water. So does a growing Maun. So do swelling cattle herds. A plan is afoot to dredge a channel in the lower delta to increase the flow downstream. Many who fear destruction of the delicate marsh ecosystem ask whether it might be safer to tap the Okavango in the Panhandle, by routing a pipeline around the delta. A pipeline, though, is expensive even for diamond money. Foreign aid? Perhaps. Foreign environmentalists argue that unique ecosystems are the heritage of humankind, but is humankind willing to pay for them?

In Botswana the future of water and wilderness intertwine like the delta's channels. In 1988 the nation's human population growth was 3.5 percent. At that rate the population doubles *every 20 years*. Sooner or later, drought will come again. How many more people, how many more cattle will need water when it does?

A small incident back in Maun reminded me how keenly attuned this land is to water. The rains were tapering off for the year, but that evening a drenching shower had struck, drumming for a while on the veranda roof outside Riley's Hotel. In the dining room the headwaiter, a Motswana, paused to chat at our table and not, as might happen elsewhere, to apologize to visitors for the weather. "We were enjoying the rain outside," he said, and added sadly, "It has stopped now, but it was very nice."

By Jonathan B. Tourtellot
Photographs by Frans Lanting

Europe

By the time the national park idea was conceived in the late 19th century, most land in Europe was spoken for. By then many of the ecosystems surviving in western Europe—the Atlantic grassland, the heather moor—had already been modified by man. The steppes of eastern Europe had been broken by the plow, and much of the boreal forest had been transformed as well. One of the few places wilderness remained was in Scandinavia, and it was there, in the far north of Sweden, that two of the first European national parks—Abisko and Peljekajse—were created in 1909. Switzerland followed with its Swiss National Park near Zernez in 1914. (The founding principle of that first Swiss park—absolute noninterference with natural processes—was ahead of its time.)

There is far more wildness in the national parks of Europe than the New World chauvinist might imagine. Brown bears live in the Western Pyrénées National Park of France, lynx in the mountain parks of Yugoslavia, wolves and imperial eagles in the Extremadura of Spain. In Abruzzo National Park in Italy's Apennines, just two hours' drive from Rome, live bears, chamois, and wolves. (There are no wild wolves within two hours of Detroit or New York City.)

Tatra National Park in Poland protects relict forests of stone pine, of dwarf mountain pine, and of mountain spruce. Mikri Prespa National Park in Greece preserves wetlands in that nation's north, a last refuge of a number of rare Adriatic birds. On an island in the Baltic, a Swedish national park known as Gotska Sandön mediates, without taking sides, in the ancient fight between the island's pine forests and the shifting dunes of its coast.

The natural history of Yugoslavia is as thoroughly balkanized as the linguistic or political history of that Balkan nation. Several vegetation zones meet in Yugoslavia—the Mediterranean and alpine, the grassland and coniferous forest, among others—and more than 5,000 plant species are native to the country.

France

La Vanoise National Park

Gondolas whisk tourists from the town of Tignes up into the Graian Alps of southeastern France. Ski lifts, inns, restaurants, and other amenities dot the periphery of La Vanoise National Park—France's first, founded in 1963. But in its heartland, an unspoiled wilderness of 200 square miles, ibex and chamois roam freely among wildflowers, lakes, glaciers, and forested mountains. More than a hundred peaks rise 9,500 feet or higher.

The first Yugoslav national park, Pelister, was established in 1949 and protects relict stands of Macedonian pine. The second, Plitvice Lakes, was founded soon after. The wonder of Plitvice is its travertine. That porous rock, created when dissolved carbonates precipitate from the region's clear streams, forms dams across waterways. The dams back up lakes. The lakes, connected by cascades and waterfalls, march down, step by step, from forests of fir, spruce, beech, and pine to the meadows of Mediterranean lowland.

Europe is the first industrialized continent on earth. It is, at the same time, the planet's most intensely developed agricultural region, and one of the most densely populated. Europeans have become, of necessity, skillful land-use planners.

Europeans are leading the way in restoration of damaged ecosystems. Ibex from Gran Paradiso National Park in Italy have been used to restock other alpine areas. To cull and revitalize populations of red deer, the lynx (once a vanished predator) has been released in the Swiss National Park. Populations of beaver, sable, elk, and a sheeplike antelope called *saiga* are rebounding in the national parks and nature reserves of the Soviet Union. Europe's most remarkable feat of restoration has been reforestation. At the turn of this century, most western European forests were gone. France was only 6 percent forested, Germany not much better. Today much of western Europe has been replanted in dense stands of trees. The restored forests are not immune to air pollution and other environmental insults, of course. *Waldsterben*, the forest death that strips trees of needles and leaves, and damages roots and branches, is rampant in the evergreens, oaks, and birches of Germany's Black Forest and in Bayerischer Wald National Park. Germany's success in counteracting Waldsterben may signify how green our future will be.

It is fitting that Europe, where industrial man began, is showing the way.

Spain

Doñana National Park

In elegant formation, hundreds of flamingos pass over the marshlands of Doñana National Park. At the confluence of African and European migration routes, this sanctuary shelters countless thousands of birds, including the rare Spanish imperial eagle. Nearly half of Europe's bird species live here or pass through on their semiannual journeys.

One of Europe's last great wildernesses, Doñana was a hunting ground for Spanish kings for 500 years until set aside as a national park in 1969. Located south of Seville, at the mouth of the Guadalquivir River, Doñana's marshy delta sweeps back from a 20-mile-wide band of sand dunes. The Spanish lynx, which can hear a mouse 250 feet away, prowls among the scrubby pines and cork oaks. Overhead soar imperial eagles, bestowing their noble presence on this regal paradise.

113

Italy

Abruzzo National Park

Gray wolves stand sentinel on the rocks of their enclosure in Civitella Alfedena, one of five villages in Abruzzo National Park. Spread over nearly 154 square miles, the park straddles the Apennines mountain chain. Beech and pine forests cloak the mountains' lower slopes; many of the beeches are several hundred years old.

Of Italy's five national parks, Abruzzo boasts the most varied wildlife. Chamois and deer graze its alpine meadows, and the European brown bear—saved from extinction—now roams in healthy numbers. Wolves, foxes, and wildcats stalk the woods, which are also home to peregrine falcons and golden eagles.

In the park's center lies the winter resort of Pescasseroli. Here, among the ski lifts and rental chalets, conservationists battle with developers over Abruzzo's future.

A. Bardi, Panda Photo

Italy

Gran Paradiso National Park

Larches line a valley in Gran Paradiso National Park, once a royal hunting reserve. Gran Paradiso's alpine landscape lies in northwestern Italy, in the shadow of France's imposing Mont Blanc range.

In 1856 King Victor Emmanuel II established a hunting reserve here to protect the last hundred ibex living in Europe. These crescent-horned antelope had been hunted almost to extinction, due in part to superstition: A tiny bone in the ibex's heart had long been sought as a lucky charm.

Today more than 3,000 ibex and 5,000 chamois range over the park. Ermines, marmots, and badgers prowl its meadows, and 80 species of birds—including golden eagles, alpine swifts, snow finches, and ptarmigan—nest in the area.

Iceland

Thingvellir National Park

Clouds of steam billow from
hot springs on the rocky banks
of Thingvallavatn, Iceland's
largest lake. Here, deep in a
mountain-ringed valley, Thingvellir National Park hugs the
lake's northern shore. The
park straddles the Mid-Atlantic
Ridge, where the Eurasian and
North American tectonic plates
meet. Plate movements widen
the valley at an average rate of
almost half an inch a year.

In 1928 Thingvellir was declared a national park, a sanctuary for the nation. Revered in
medieval Norse sagas, Thingvellir is a place of mystical significance to Icelanders. The
country's first Althing, or parlia-
ment, met here in A.D. 930,
when Norse chiefs gathered
on the rugged plains to resolve
their differences, and it was
here that the Icelandic republic

Bayerischer Wald
National Park

A stand of fir trees in the Bayerischer Wald, or Bavarian Forest, recalls the unbroken woods that once covered almost all of Europe. Today trees still cloak all but one percent of Bayerischer Wald's 50 square miles. Declared Germany's first national park in 1970, it is flanked by the Danube River to the west and the Czech border to the east.

Three zones protect the park's ecosystems: one for tourists on the outer edge; an intermediate wilderness area with 80 miles of hiking trails; and, at the heart of the park, a high-altitude zone kept free from tourism and logging. Red deer, however, have damaged some 7,500 acres by stripping bark from trees. Acid rain poses an even worse threat, and the park has mounted a number of exhibits to alert the public to Germany's continuing *Waldsterben,* or forest death.

Pallas-Ounastunturi
National Park

A blanket of cotton grass unfolds in the third largest of Finland's 22 national parks. Founded in 1938 in the northwestern part of the country, Pallas-Ounastunturi embraces 193 square miles of fells, forests, heaths, and marshes. In this harsh land north of the Arctic Circle, snow often does not melt until July. During the short growing season, wildflowers blanket the banks of streams and rivers. Insects thrive, a feast for bluethroats, dotterels, Lapland buntings, and other birds.

Nomadic Saami (known to outsiders as Lapps) graze reindeer in the park and enjoy traditional hunting and fishing rights. At the park's southern edge lies an old fishing village whose wooden cabins are still used in season by locals. Fishing is also popular among visitors, as are hiking and skiing.

Sweden

Sarek National Park

Silver with silt from many glaciers, the Rapaälven River
swings through a valley of
birch forest. Though Sarek National Park encompasses 760
square miles of heaths and
meadows, glaciated peaks and
rugged valleys, only a few
thousand visitors come each
year to this corner of northwestern Sweden, the wildest
and least accessible part of the
country's 300-million-year-old
mountain chain. Most of the
park lies above the tree line,
guarded by imposing plateaus
2,000 to 3,000 feet high.

Saami use the land for grazing herds of reindeer and for
hunting and fishing. (Only
Saami may hunt and fish in the
park.) Brown bears, lynx, foxes, wolverines, and elk also
roam the parkland; gyrfalcons,
white-fronted geese, and gold-
en eagles soar over its crags
and wetlands.

A view along Wasdale to Wast Water gives truth to William Wordsworth's words about England's Lake District: "I do not indeed know of any tract of country in which, within so narrow a compass, may be found an equal variety in the influences of light and shadow upon the sublime or beautiful features of landscape."

A Hill Country Journey

My journey round the Lake District ends at the point where it began, and there's no doubt what astonishes me most about this English conjuring act, this remarkable box of scenic tricks. It is magical, using the word in a literal and sober rather than a travelogue sense. Clearly nothing changes fundamentally, in the long term, and yet I now also know that nothing stays the same —not for a day, often not for an hour on end. Come here a hundred times, you won't see the same view twice.

I find it hard to believe that this is where my journey began, on a murky day three weeks ago, here by this slightly moldering jetty at the weedy southwest corner of Coniston Water. Then, the scene was opaque as the leaden lake and sky; you could scarcely see the Old Man of Coniston, the lake's guardian mountain, a few miles away and all of 2,600 feet high.

Now, 20 days deeper into the fall (the seasons themselves put on a magic act and seem to go backwards), it's another place. The water sparkles, affable white clouds drift around the sky in summery fashion, the Old Man (illusion again) is not only there but looks a mere ten minutes' walk away. An hour or so (sheer fantasy) to the top, and from there they promise you can see wonders like the Isle of Man, Blackpool Tower, even the tip of Snowdon perhaps.

Or one may prefer, as I'm doing at present, just to sit back and enjoy the view, a relaxed and splendid prospect looking northward up the lake. It is a serene autumn day with not a soul in sight; you'd never think that behind the screening trees, and all down the shore of nearby Windermere, the tourists from across the world are still speeding in their cars. "They stretched in never-ending line. . . ." If a modern Wordsworth made that observation, it wouldn't be daffodils he was writing about, even if they happened to be in season. Nor would one be

Lake District National Park

880 Square Miles

In the county of Cumbria, the second largest in England, lies Lake District National Park. From the high, craggy peaks at the center of the park, a pinwheel of mountains ("fells," in local parlance), valleys (dales), and lakes (meres and tarns) radiates outward. Lakeland landscape was raised by volcanic eruptions, folded by tectonic movement, washed by an ancient sea, carved by Ice Age glaciers. Inspired by the dramatic scenery were such 18th- and 19th-century poets as William Wordsworth, Robert Southey, and Samuel Taylor Coleridge, who became known as the Lake Poets. The national park encompasses the heart of the Lake District region.

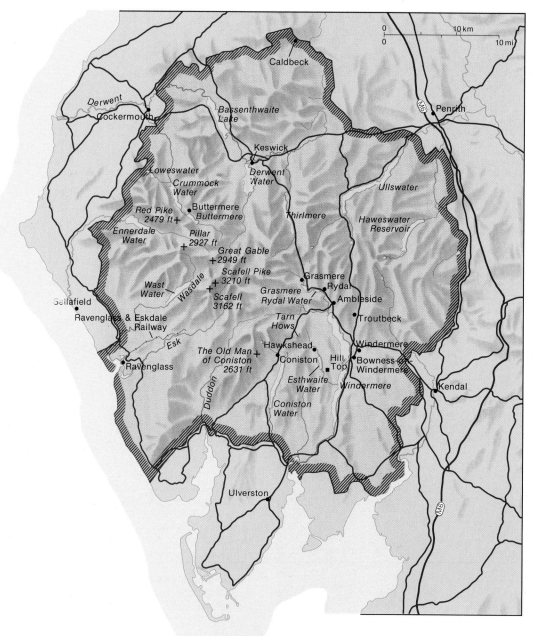

William Wordsworth's sister, Dorothy, lies beside the poet's son and his wife, Fanny, at St. Oswald's Parish Church in Grasmere, a town where Wordsworth lived for 14 years. He wrote of the church, behind which he too is buried: "Not raised in nice proportions was the pile, But large and massy; for duration built. . . ."

inclined to recall that it was on this peaceful lake that Donald Campbell somersaulted to his death in 1967 trying to beat his own world water-speed record in a jet-powered boat. Coniston had grown accustomed by then to the roar of the record breakers.

Such contrasts and contradictions are routine form. Modern times have left their mark even here, as the Old Man as well as the lake are well aware. "Coniston without its Old Man is unthinkable," remarks A. Wainwright, prince of fell-walking guides, who is also understandably concerned about what has happened to the revered oldest inhabitant. The Old Man has been severely battered—scarred by quarries and mine workings, mugged not so much by the gods and the elements as by man. Some will see them as honorable scars. Men have to work and why not mountains, many would say. And above and beyond these old industrial wounds, all is a visual wonderland. (You don't *have* to look at Blackpool Tower.)

To real mountaineers, of course, climbing a Lakeland mountain is like walking up stairs. (Not that they sneer; several world-class operators have lived and climbed here for pleasure and practice.) But these lakes and fells make up in sheer theatricality what they lack in dimension. Windermere, the biggest lake, is just over ten miles long, and the highest local mountains barely top three thousand feet, mere pimples and puddles by international measure. Yet they manage—by sheer stagecraft as it were—to conjure up scene after scene of immense grandeur and beauty, constantly changing, a nonstop variety act that brings back the holidaymakers and tourists again and again.

Suitably clad, needless to say. They know that this scenic appeal is Lakeland's compensation for its weather; indeed, without its weather the show couldn't really go on. And the weather, it has to be admitted, can be abominable. Or rather, it needn't be admitted because there is a strong and sensible convention in these parts (almost alone

Rain dampens streets but not spirits at the first outing of the season for the Blencathra Hunt. Like five other hunts in the Lake District, where terrain is often hilly and rough, the Blencathra is horseless. Hunters and hounds set forth on foot; spectators follow on foot or in cars. As one local hunting song goes:

*Who'd hunt the fox with
    spur and rein?
Away, away!
To have a mount we'd all
    disdain,
Away, my lads, away!*

in weather-conscious Britain) that this is a subject you don't discuss. When the glass is low, it rains. When the glass rises, as like as not it still rains. You can't get away from it, so you don't talk about it. You put up your umbrella or adjust your rain hood and await the switch-off. Cumbrian rain seems to turn on and off as if by a giant tap, and storm effects are common. This adds to the theatrical aura: You think of the weatherman waiting there in the wings, flashes and thunder sheet at the ready.

One can't help feeling that William Wordsworth, who spent so much of his time wandering around these hills and lakeside paths, must have been one of the wettest poets in literary history; but there was always a sister or wife, if not both, to dry him off when he got home. If he could come back to Grasmere and Rydal, he would find it less easy to take those contemplative walks round the home lakes; he would need to watch his back. Yet the prospects that so deeply moved him and nourished his thoughts and his work are still there.

Few among the Wordsworth-hunting multitudes seem to have much idea at all about what the man actually *wrote*—apart, of course, from "Daffodils," and even that wouldn't have happened (as we learn from sister Dorothy's journal) if they hadn't been trying to avoid some cows. One doesn't expect tourists to go around clutching *The Excursion* under their arms, but they would do well to realize that if Wordsworth revived anything, it was simplicity and plain language. He wrote about real people with real feelings and unromantic afflictions like old age and weak ankles, not to mention a grinding poverty that held many of them in its grip. You can meet their like still, though the poverty may have eased. Come to think of it, the Wordsworths themselves were often cold and sick as well as damp.

And they were poor enough in the earlier days before the poet accepted the official post of Distributor of Stamps for the County of Westmorland, an unromantic but reasonably lucrative revenue job. The coarse truth is that poets have to live, and so do their wives and children, and they don't live on daffodils. Wordsworth trackers might get nearer to the man, and the poet too, if they looked for the local life and interests which he shared, and which even tourism hasn't swamped out of existence.

I was lucky. Coming through Coniston village, dodging the traffic in its twisting streets, I happened on a scene that would certainly have been recorded by William in verse, or Dorothy in prose, if not both. There had been a wedding in the church, and pictures were being taken outside—a familiar enough village scene. Except that this was a hunting wedding; hounds as well as bridesmaids posed before the cameras, a fox's tail ("brush" to them) flickered among the bouquets, a hunting horn sounded out a weird ululation after the last organ notes had died away. An ancient villager who was watching told me of the days when guests rode to weddings, two on a horse, and sometimes fell off going home.

Wordsworth's own progression, if that is the word, from youthful visionary to voice of reaction, *Lyrical Ballads* to Lakeland guide, French Revolution admirer to county tax collector, may be distinctly unromantic, but it accords well enough with the local spirit of self-contradiction. That successful guidebook of his, *A Description of the Scenery of the Lakes in the North of England,* was published in 1822 and indicates that the Lake District cult was established earlier than you might think. And if the multitudes had to be welcomed to the solitudes, why shouldn't a needy poet carve himself a slice of the action?

However little things may have changed fundamentally, it would be eccentric, though certainly fascinating, for a modern tourist to steer himself round the Lakes with the help of the Wordsworth guide. Some of the main attractions, of course, would not be recorded. How could they be? It would be not unlike finding a long-lost *Shakespeare's Guide to Stratford.* Doing my own devoted round of the various Wordsworth shrines, I wondered what it can be that we look for in such places. Clearly not the works; this is neither the time nor the place for attending to blank verse. Not the portraits, impressive as they are, growing steadily more ceremonious as they climb ever grander walls. It must be the domestic bits and pieces—the great man's skates, his picnic box, the picture of his dog Pepper given him by his friend Sir Walter Scott. Things like that.

But nothing here is so moving as the schoolhouse at Hawkshead—moving, imaginative in its handling or rather unhandling, more than a shade eerie. The young Wordsworth learned his lessons in this school. It stands silent and empty much of the year, a sort of architectural spook. Nothing seems changed—the master's stern desk, the lowly benches of the pupils with their carved names, including the young William's. Only one thing has been added: Round the cornice are painted texts from the poems. I couldn't help imagining the ghost of a small boy sitting at the desk he occupied two centuries ago, looking down at his own signature he had cut in the oak, gazing up at the famous words he was yet to write: "The Child is Father of the Man." This was indeed the child who had sired the whole enterprise.

I can't think of a spookier place, unless it is the Laurel and Hardy shrine at Ulverston, less than 20 miles south as the cuckoo flies. Some mistake, surely? Not at all. Stan Laurel was born there, and the Sons of the Desert (the Laurel and Hardy Appreciation Society) come from all over the world to visit what is in effect a museum, information center, and temple of devotion rolled into one. Devotion is devotion, whether directed toward great poets or great clowns. In one respect the clowns may have the edge.

Tourists have been known in Grasmere to ask what this guy Wordsworth did. There's no record of the question ever having been asked in Ulverston about Laurel.

Whether the celebrated pair, when in England, ever took time off for a walk over Stan's native hills seems doubtful. The moodiness of this landscape can certainly accommodate clowns and poets alike, and there's a bit of both in the temperament of Cumbrians, who are inclined to a boisterousness that is sometimes sunny, sometimes dark. Landscape, it often seems to me, probably affects regional temperaments more than is commonly supposed.

This brings one to an aspect of the Cumbrian scene the guidebooks don't much dwell on—a sometimes sinister air, a capacity to alarm. Which may be just as well, since even these mini-mountains have their perils. Those strategically positioned ambulance posts aren't there just to thrill the tourists. Mountain rescue teams, in fact, go into action several hundred times a year, with perhaps two dozen deaths.

Sudden mists can be fatal. Sudden squalls too. An old editor of mine was drowned in a sailing accident on Windermere. Up in the hills you come across warning signs like the one I found on Coniston Old Man: "There are many old mines and quarries on these fells including dangerous deep shafts in unstable ground." You have to watch your step, and other people's step too.

Fair seed-time had my soul, and I grew up
Fostered alike by beauty and by fear. . . .
Wordsworth wrote that in *The Prelude*. Beauty and fear. He was frightened by the mountains as a child and wrote about his fear in memorable retrospective verse, describing how an apparently harmless hill reared up, grew huge, chased him "like a living thing." What could be more terrifying than that? A post-Freudian analyst would have had him down at sea level almost before his back had left the couch; but Wordsworth stuck it out, perhaps even enjoyed it

in the perverse way poets happily have. His essential love of the hill country was in no way damaged. Maybe it was enhanced.

The day I saw Esthwaite and its attendant hills, like those which are supposed to have put the frighteners on young Wordsworth, buttercups wouldn't have melted in its mouth. I found it hiding away rather coyly between Windermere and Coniston, both of which were looking as good as gold in the sunshine, while Esthwaite's own mood was positively benign. This seemed appropriate since I was about to call on Mrs. William Heelis at Hill Top, just at the end of the lake —or rather the unfading memory of this lady, who is otherwise and better known as Beatrix Potter, writer and farmer. Some years, her house attracts as many visitors as Wordsworth's Dove Cottage, which seems only fair; no doubt *The Tale of Peter Rabbit* still finds more readers than *The Prelude*. It is equally, in its different field, a work of unfading genius.

Yet she was being rewritten at the time, reillustrated even, starting a row that got into the national editorials. People felt strongly about it. (I actually found the new version being offered for sale at nearby Brantwood, John Ruskin's house. One woman visitor was so appalled that she was surreptitiously hiding copies of the heretical version behind other books in the hope they wouldn't be seen.) There'd been nothing like the vehemence this enterprise aroused since they rewrote the Bible. If people still delighted in the originals, as obviously they did, why offer them substitutes? I couldn't think of an answer.

Back at Hill Top, I had a question that I couldn't bring myself to ask. Having written her most famous stories, Beatrix Potter became a professional hill farmer, by all accounts formidably efficient at the job. It was an embarrassing and rather painful thought, but did she, in that highly practical capacity, actually *shoot* Peter Rabbits? If not, she must have been about the only farmer around the Lakes who didn't. It was a suspicion you kept to yourself at Hill Top. But I did see a gun there. . . .

Another famous literary figure who fell in love with the Lakes was Samuel Taylor Coleridge, Wordsworth's friend and collaborator in the early *Lyrical Ballads,* which included his *Ancient Mariner,* one of the eeriest poems of all time. When younger, Coleridge was at least as enthusiastic a fell walker as Wordsworth, and they went on a walking tour together in 1799. Coleridge also liked going on long and arduous expeditions alone, and reportedly climbed some of the highest peaks.

He certainly knew Buttermere, tucked away in its secluded valley to the northwest. Walking the fells here is strenuous, but its reward in magnificent views and sheer physical exhilaration would be hard to beat. Anyone seeking a microcosm of the whole region, the Lakes in little, need go no farther. (Often people don't; they return to Buttermere year after year.) At first I found these lakes artfully living up to their names —Buttermere looking bland and softish, Crummock Water on the dour side. An hour later, in true Lakeland fashion, they had switched characters before my eyes.

And soon the variety show was starting. I saw a rainbow reflected in Buttermere, lying on the surface as if it had fallen out of the sky. There was my piece of magic for the day; surely nothing was going to beat that. Then I saw a cormorant flying across Crummock Water. This worried me; I wasn't at all sure it ought to have happened. Cormorants belonged to the sea, didn't they? Myth dies hard here. Perhaps they hadn't forgotten Coleridge and his albatross. Perhaps Cumbrians were tired of strangers coming here and seeing things. Still, one had to know.

"I thought I saw a cormorant," I nervously mentioned to a man in Buttermere village. He showed no surprise, not much interest at all; so that was all right.

Built from the same rock they stand on, thousands of miles of dry-stone walls pattern the Lake District landscape. Some say there is no better countryside in the world for walking excursions. Wordsworth, who spent years exploring Lakeland on foot, wrote of this area around Troutbeck: "There is scarcely a field on the road side, which, if entered, would not give to the landscape some additional charm."

In Loweswater, a rather pretty lake and the smallest of this group, two men and a boy were fishing for trout. I watched one being hooked and played without excitement, even on the boy's part. They were very casual about it all. Six is quite a good day's catch, they told me; twelve would be "a bit of a record." I remembered Wordsworth's sister recording that she and some friends caught thirteen bass in Grasmere in one day and that she and William ate stuffed pike from the lakes—a touch of high living and plain thinking for a change?

It was Sunday morning when I made my reluctant farewells to Buttermere. There was a clutter of cars on the narrow road leading out of the village. Not another pile-up—not here? It was a day for blood sports all right, but not human blood. People were gazing up the fellside, many of them with field glasses. After a few minutes we saw a hunt go by—stroll by, you might have said. Hunting here is on foot, and this looked a quiet enough affair—placid even, like a Sunday morning walk with the dogs. No doubt things would liven up dramatically if they came anywhere near a fox, but I didn't wait for that. I couldn't help wishing them bad hunting.

I was determined to visit the remoter lakes, Ennerdale and Wast Water; and so potent was the aura I was feeling or imagining that it really began to seem a project of difficulty and challenge, a journey not to be undertaken lightly. And then I was struck by the absurdity of the idea. Scarcely more than five miles as the crow or raven flies, but you'd think it was another country.

Wast Water? People I consulted in Buttermere had looked dubious, as though we were discussing one of the less frequented corners of the Kalahari Desert. As for getting there, the only thing I gathered was that I really ought to be starting from somewhere else. Indeed, I discovered that the comparatively few tourists who seek out the western lakes usually do it the strangest

A woolly crowd of black-masked Swaledales assembles for a dip in a chemical that controls mites and ticks. Today's quick dunk is one of many veterinary improvements in the ancient Lakeland profession of sheep farming. Dipping replaced tedious salving with a rancid mixture of butter and tar.

Lakeland tourists seeking comforts of home along with the view will likely find both in resort towns like Ambleside (left) and Bowness (lower left) on the shores of Windermere, England's largest and most popular lake. Those looking to discover the true character of the Lakes will do better to choose the more remote Buttermere (opposite), where the passage of an hour or two might result in a dramatic change of scene (next pages) so typical of the Lake District.

way. They take a circuitous route to the coast, then strike back inland as though planning to move in on their objective unawares. It shows not only how complicated travel can be in this small corner of England —the whole national park is only 30 miles across—but also how the automobile has actually lengthened journeys in these paradoxical parts. Treks that were once short if arduous are now achieved by car in huge strategic circles.

With the M6 Motorway bringing a third of the population within a few hours' reach, and increasing numbers of visitors achieving their tour of the Lakes without getting out of their cars, it may soon be necessary to rethink Lake District transport on radical lines. From feet back to feet in how many generations? We may know earlier than we think. After the first feet came the hooves: Fell ponies, much used by the early holidaymakers as well as local travelers, are said to be on the way back, though none crossed

A climber (opposite) descends with greater ease than did Samuel Taylor Coleridge in 1802, when he scrambled unaided down a rocky face on Scafell; the poet's report of his precipitous descent added to the early annals of rock-climbing. Lakeland adventurers leery of hanging from ropes may prefer tunneling through abandoned quarries in total darkness (above).

my path. Other old faithfuls are still with us, and a few new ones. I did see a mountain goat service advertised; this turned out to be a herd of minibuses. Steam trains survive in two valleys, and steamboats on several of the lakes; I happily accepted a cruise on an opulent steam yacht called *Gondola,* vintage 1859, rescued and imaginatively renovated (complete with gleaming Victorian saloons) by the National Trust.

But how was I to get to Ennerdale? How to get to Wast Water? Five miles as the raven flies, but a world away. Steam yachts don't fly, any more than automobiles. The shortest way remained Coleridge's way. Ask him how to get from Buttermere to Ennerdale, a lake he much admired, and he would have pointed over Red Pike—surprised, no doubt, that you should have found it necessary to ask the question—and expected to see you start walking.

The shortest, the healthiest, the most beautiful and exhilarating, the obvious and

indeed the only way: the direct hill track with stupendous views. Who, against this, would choose the circuitous coastal route?

I did, feeling appropriately guilty. I persuaded myself to choose the coastal route because I wanted to see Ravenglass. This old Roman seaport was still important in the Middle Ages. It became notorious for quicksands and smugglers; but eventually ships turned their backs and so did the guidebook writers, who for the most part pay Ravenglass scant attention. It deserves better. It struck me as a strange and fascinating little place, this port that has lost its sea trade but retained some of the most remarkable Roman ruins I know of. Nobody seems to guard them. Perhaps the vandals never got as far as this.

Having lost its past, indeed a number of pasts, where does Ravenglass look now? Here the story takes on a decidedly weird air. The place still runs a little steam train, and this links to a service for people wanting to see the nuclear reprocessing plant just up the coast at Sellafield. "It's just one step from the Railway Age to the Nuclear Age," a leaflet proclaims. There is said to be a nuclear age intelligentsia living in the area who enjoy civilized leisure activities like Beethoven quartets.

And so—traveling north and east now to finish my journey west—at last to Ennerdale Water. Obviously it has changed since Coleridge gave it so much praise. I found it as austere as one had been led to expect, but it seems as much a man-made as a natural austerity. Armies of well-disciplined conifers have advanced on it in recent years, and the sergeant major never looks far away ("Strictly no swimming or boating").

But Wast Water made up for it. I found it an awesome place. This is authentic Edgar Allan Poe territory; if one ever heard a bird say "Nevermore," it would surely be here. I was not at all surprised that there should be ravens, nor are they apparently averse from uttering. Wordsworth has one with a voice

Wagers made and binoculars in position, spectators follow a hound trail, or dog race, at the Wasdale Show, one of many annual Lakeland sports events. For the more athletically inclined: a tug-of-war. The truly ambitious might join in a fell race, running up and down a mountain in a breakneck display of stamina and daring.

like "an iron knell" echoing and reechoing through the hills. It would take a bold spirit to swim in this lake; surely it would be unbearably cold even in a heat wave. A bottomless lake it looks, guarded by giants —Scafell, Great Gable, Pillar.

"This is the most forbidding scene of all the Lake District" was the reaction of one writer, Doreen Wallace. Lacking Poe, Tennyson would go well here with his magical sword act, the arm coming out of the lake to catch King Arthur's abandoned sword Excalibur. In fact, this scene may belong to one of the more northern lakes, Bassenthwaite, where Tennyson (clearly in gloomy mood) was staying with a friend. Today Bassenthwaite is favored by yachtsmen, and mystic arms thrusting out of the water, clothed in white samite or anything else, would be frowned upon as a hazard to sailing.

Wast Water is a favorite base for serious walkers and climbers. Also, the nearby dales provide the best insight the region can

offer into the traditional Lakeland way of life and the Cumbrian temperament—a contrasting, often baffling mixture of grimness and jollity. Cumbrians go in for a particularly macabre line in folk legends, specializing in gruesome tales about witches, specters on the corpse roads across the fells, and haunted halls and farmsteads.

Go to one of their dalesmen's shows, concentrating on Herdwick sheep but offering much else besides, and you'll find the farmers relaxing into their earthy and somewhat enigmatical line of fun. An announcer makes a series of impenetrable domestic jokes which bring the house down, then one or two of more general appeal. A purse has been found. Somebody has left their teeth in the refreshment tent (this they find hilarious). The announcer sings "John Peel" at the top of his voice, not pedantically in tune. (Incidentally, the famous huntsman never lived at Troutbeck "once on a day" or any time at all; he lived at Caldbeck, some miles to the north.) Would he have taken part in the parade that now follows to select "the best-dressed huntsman"?

There is a parade of foxhounds with names John Peel might have called—Bellman, Tramper, Trueman; then a parade of hunt terriers; then, their movements like quicksilver, the wonderful shepherds' dogs. Angular young men, all brawny legs and elbows, set off on the fell race. Everything is itself, individual, different. Their races are perpendicular, not horizontal like everybody else's. Their hunting is on foot. Their sheep are a different build and can withstand long burial in snowdrifts. Their wrestling, static and muscle cracking, looks like a conflict of giants or minor mountains. They do things as nobody else does them.

Back at Coniston, the place where I began which is so different from that place, I feel I have traveled a long way these few miles. I have circled the Lake District anticlockwise to discover, in the end, some such truth as that this region is traveling by steam train into the nuclear age.

Its traditional industries go on, diminishingly. Cumbrians still farm, quarry, mine a little. Tourism can't be withstood nor would anyone want to try; it is the major fact of this region's life, and a living partnership—a balance of interests which are in the end the same interest—has to be maintained.

Yet mountains and lakes as playgrounds are not enough, however well supervised. A Lake District National Park can be no mere conservation area, still less any kind of static or even working museum. Not all the cash flowing in from the tourists, nor the standards so well maintained by the National Trust, which owns key parts of the park, can amount to much if a genuine organic life doesn't pulse on beneath the well-cared-for skin. The region, as far as I could tell, seemed to be surviving. Alive, if precariously. Which of us can say more?

By Norman Shrapnel
Photographs by Ian Berry

Both man and time have altered the wooded banks of Tarn Hows: Landowners at the turn of the 20th century joined three natural pools to form the lake and planted shoreline trees. Everywhere in the Lake District, grazing, industry, and the feet of millions of tourists have taken a toll. But in spite of all, most of the rugged landscape endures, like Tarn Hows, unspoiled if not untouched.

Backed by the forested slopes of the Caucasus Mountains, a warden rides home from patrol to field headquarters in Kavkaz reserve. Most Soviet nature reserves prohibit tourism, but Kavkaz allows the public in to enjoy its scenic beauty.

Soviet Union

Astrakhan' State Nature Reserve

Kavkaz State Nature Reserve

Prioksko-Terrasnyy State Nature Reserve

Guarding Nature's Heritage

The patrol camp is a floating shed anchored among islands of reed and lotus in the shallow northern end of the Caspian Sea. Inside, the teakettle is whistling. Overhead, waves of migrating birds squall across a gray sky. Fishermen call the wind here "hole-in-hat" for the way its chill seems to blow straight through you. Soon, it whispers, the white-tailed sea eagles will be hunting swans in pools surrounded by ice. Wolves will pad out to wait by breathing holes for young seals. And the guards of Astrakhan' reserve will strap on skates to patrol the same channels and bays we just traveled by boat.

"I am as fast on my feet as a younger man then," Vasiliy Shkvarnikov, age 62, smiles through the steam from his tea mug. "In four hours I can reach this camp from headquarters and return." A trip of 30 miles, it sometimes leads across ice panes so clear he can watch blizzards of fish racing beneath his feet. Each of us deserves a job like that for a while: guarding nature while she practices magic. At the very least, each of us deserves to know a bit more about conservation in the largest of modern superpowers, the Soviet Union. I was given a chance to learn about it firsthand when I visited three key examples of the most carefully protected category of wildlands in the U.S.S.R. These are the refuges called *zapovedniki,* or state nature reserves.

In old Russia, as elsewhere in Europe, the earliest reserves were hunting parks for the aristocracy. The tsar set aside more ground in the 17th century, trying to save for himself a small, forest-dwelling fortune in fur—the sable, decimated by trapping. Early in the 20th century, much as in the United States, Russian scientists and conservationists began to press for a national

145

Soviet State Nature Reserves

Astrakhan' 244 Square Miles; Kavkaz 1,017 Square Miles; Prioksko-Terrasnyy 19 Square Miles

SOVIET UNION

The Soviet Union covers 8.6 million square miles and provides habitats ranging from arctic tundra to subtropical desert for its abundant plant and animal species. In 1916, the year the National Park Service was established in the United States, Russian law authorized the creation of protected areas that foreshadowed today's *zapovedniki*—state nature reserves. Squares on the map locate the three discussed here. Unlike U. S. parks, Soviet reserves are set aside for ecological studies, and tourism usually is not permitted. Bison are bred at Prioksko-Terrasnyy; migrating waterfowl are banded in the wetlands of Astrakhan'; and Kavkaz harbors plant species several million years old.

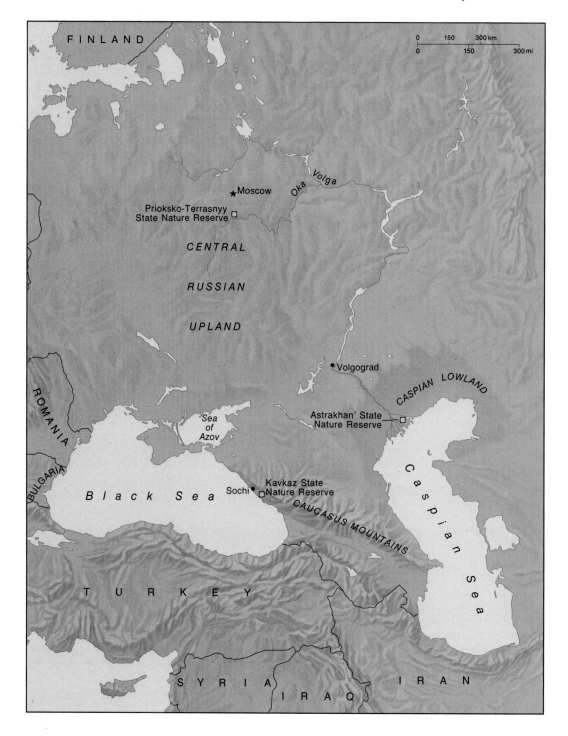

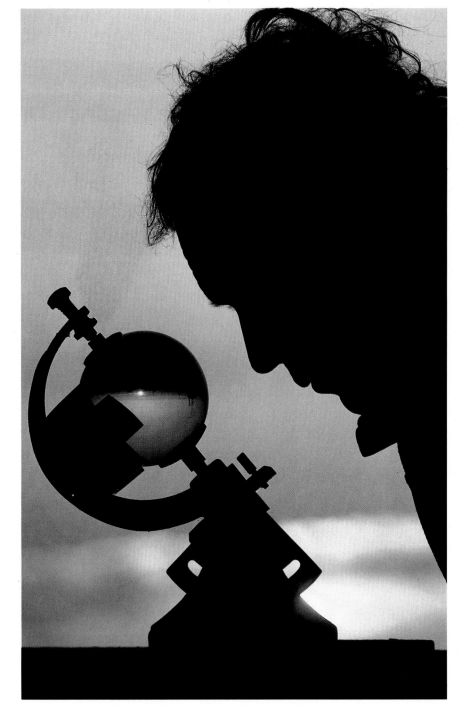

system of parks and nature reserves. Two or three were established by 1916.

In 1919 Vladimir Ilich Lenin was in the midst of hammering out a new state without tsars when Nikolai Podyapolskiy came to call, representing fellow citizens from the Astrakhan' district. Podyapolskiy wanted to talk about the state of the Volga River Delta. Market hunters were plundering its bird populations. Stocks of fish, which included most of the nation's caviar-producing sturgeon, were being squandered apace. Lenin agreed to help create Astrakhan' reserve from three separate segments of the delta. He also directed Podyapolskiy to draft legislation for a national system of reserves along with strict measures for guarding them.

Astrakhan' thus marked the beginning of the Soviet zapovedniki system. These areas have since increased to more than 150. Half were established in just the past 30 years. The number is expected to increase considerably by the turn of this century. Ultimately, planners say, there will be at least one such reserve to represent every variety of biological community found in the U.S.S.R. That is saying a great deal for a nation extending across 11 time zones to take in one-sixth of the planet's land surface.

From Uzbekistan, where desert tortoises cross the tracks of wild asses in the dunes, to Kamchatka, where great brown bears snag salmon at the drizzly edge of the Pacific, the purpose of the state nature reserves remains constant: to safeguard plants, animals, and ecosystems while scientists carry out continuous, detailed studies. Activities other than research, management of rare or endangered species, and patrol duties are generally prohibited. That means little or no economic use. No tourists, either, except in a few older reserves, and therein lies a fundamental difference from U. S. parks and refuges. A zapovednik is intended to serve as a standard of nature—a control against which human influences of every type, including recreation, can be measured.

But then the world is full of admirable plans on paper. How committed might the Soviet people really be to this concept of wildlands in practice? I had little idea of what to expect when I arrived.

Astrakhan' reserve's scientists include ornithologist German Rusanov, who gave up a career in aviation for the outdoor life among born flyers. His favorite author is American conservationist Aldo Leopold. "When I have troubles of the spirit," says German, "I take your Leopold off the shelf to read. He reminds me of the enduring importance of the kind of work we are doing."

Before Astrakhan' was set aside, every fashionable Cossack officer galloping into love or battle wore plumes from a great white egret in his cap. Ladies' hats, too, sprouted egret plumes. Live examples of the bird grew scarce. Only two pairs could be found within the new reserve. Mute swans (it's true they don't call, but you can hear their big angel wings making the air sigh a hundred yards off) had vanished altogether. Shot for their skins to make powder puffs, they didn't reappear here until 1936.

Today, 244-square-mile Astrakhan' reserve is one of four zapovedniki bordering the Caspian Sea. Designated a biosphere reserve in 1984 under UNESCO's Man and the Biosphere Program, it functions as headquarters for the Caspian Ornithological Station, coordinating bird marking efforts and studies throughout the region. Not long ago, German and his colleagues counted 30,000 great white egrets and 10,000 mute swans nesting in the Volga Delta—together with 14,000 greylag geese, 100,000 cormorants, and a host of other success stories.

Researchers found that excrement from the cormorant colonies, falling into the water, enriches the whole delta with nitrogen and phosphorus that promote the development of zooplankton. This is ultimately reflected in a high production of fish. And fish are what cormorants survive on. At the same time, chunks of food dropped by cormorant nestlings feed catfish lounging in springtime floodwaters below. Big catfish and pike gulp the occasional bird as well. If you believe the local stories, Volga catfish can weigh up to 300 or 400 pounds—the size of the wild boars rooting up cattails alongshore—and have even carried off young children.

Interweavings of life on a smaller scale are examined by Vladislav Sudarikov of the U.S.S.R. Academy of Sciences, one of dozens of outside specialists who conduct field research at Astrakhan'. At a log cabin laboratory on a delta island, he wriggles a parasitic worm into focus under his microscope. It was just removed from a common little fish called a stickleback. The larvae infest snails first, develop into a different larval form, then move on to sticklebacks. "In the fish, they lodge in the eye, and specifically in the upper part of the eye," Sudarikov explains. "This makes it difficult for the fish to see above itself, so it becomes that much easier for a bird to catch. The worm must have a third host as well—a grebe. It completes the last stage of its life cycle in the bird's stomach. The worm's eggs enter the water through grebe droppings, develop into larvae, invade a snail. . . ."

How can a worm be programmed for all that? I ask. "It is nature," the scientist shrugs and, to my boundless satisfaction, goes on to display a parasitic worm that bugs mosquitoes.

I help another scientist unfurl a sail of patched cloth above a slender wooden boat and point it toward the sea. From the Volga Delta, water no more than a foot or two deep pushes slowly outward across a thick apron of sediments for mile after mile into the northern Caspian. This so-called avant-delta nourishes masses of freshwater plants that in turn feed and harbor fleet after fleet of birds. I feel as if I am sailing into an earlier age when humans went more quietly amidst a great clamor of other life-forms.

Ornithologist Dmitriy Bondarev google-googles back at an incoming swirl of geese and notes down the exact number. Having done this sort of work for 23 years, he seldom needs binoculars to identify even the most distant flyers: Dalmatian pelicans, European bee eaters, lapwings, spoonbills, ferruginous pochards, squacco herons, bearded reedlings, whooper swans, a whorl of common buzzards hitchhiking on a thermal up into the clouds.

For migrating birds, the Volga Delta resembles the narrow waist of an hourglass. The travelers arrive from points such as the British Isles, France, Sweden, the Siberian tundra, funneling in with their offspring— distant algae, insects, and fish converted to new flesh and feathers—and their parasites. Some birds will stay the winter. Others will flare outward with Volga-born birds, extending this macro-ecosystem to the Mediterranean, the Nile Delta, the Red Sea, Afghanistan, and India.

Studying events of such scope seems to draw people beyond the usual boundaries of thought. "Every day we see more interrelations. And looking at things from so many points of view teaches a man to keep more open—more kind," Dmitriy believes. "We live in times when everything that surrounds some people is technical and industrial. Only in wild places like this do you begin to understand how tender life is." In wild places like this, with a Russian and an American together in a little boat, gusting like a feather over the green Caspian Sea.

The Soviet Union does have wildlands designated as national parks; by 1987 there were 18. Typically, these are created in the more accessible areas where outdoor recreation is already quite popular. Their role is to encourage tourist activities not allowed in the zapovedniki while supplying guidelines and camping facilities that will help reduce the impact of visitors. Another category, the natural monument, offers similar protection for a localized feature on the order of a lake, a spectacular rock formation, or even a single tree of historical interest.

Then come the less restrictive—and less permanent—reserves called *zakazniki,* numbering more than 2,900. They permit most human activities except those harmful to a particular resource. There are zakazniki for tigers, hot springs, and insect pollinators. There is even a zakaznik or two for lichen cited in the *Red Data Book of the U.S.S.R.*'s list of rare, threatened, and endangered species.

Part of the value of Astrakhan' and other zapovedniki is that information gathered there may reveal ways to improve management in all the other conservation categories. A state nature reserve holds in trust not only plants and animals useful to man but "those whose usefulness is still unknown." That wise phrase is from the brochure for Prioksko-Terrasnyy, a zapovednik on the terraced bank of the Oka River south of Moscow. Part of the Moscow Reserve set up in 1945, it became independent in 1948.

Glaciers rounded off the ancient river-cut terraces while depositing their own ridges of sand. From these rise pines so straight and tall they are called mast forests, ideal for shipbuilding. In this district the pine, spruce, and birch of the northern zone meet lime, oak, and maple from the broad-leaved forest zone. Intermixed with bogs, ferny grottoes, and silvery carpets of reindeer moss are some highly unusual meadows, termed *doly*. They seem to be fragments of dry, distant southern steppes that got lost in the woods. Some say their seeds must have been carried in by the north-flowing river during floods. Others think they were stowaways on Tatar military caravans that camped here. The miniature prairie environments hold up to 80 far-from-home plant species per square yard and have been luring botanists to the area since 1855.

At 19 square miles, this is not a large reserve. But with a surrounding milewide buffer zone nearly doubling the area, a

Douglas H. Chadwick

A park team explores a cormorant colony from a slender *budarka*—a fishing boat well suited to nosing through reeds and narrow channels. A sign (above) warns that the only kind of hunting allowed here in Astrakhan' is with a telescope. Although the reserve is closed to unofficial visitors, some may stray in from nearby legal hunting areas.

number of moose call the place home. So do red, or noble, deer, roe deer, wild boar, and beaver, all reintroduced after having been exterminated from the region.

The mast forests are adrift in fog this autumn morning, clammy as salamander skin and ripe with mushrooms: *dedushkin tabak*—grandfather's tobacco, a golden pouch that puffs out gray spores when the deer I'm following steps on it; *lisichka*—little fox, a rust orange toadstool; *svinushka*—pig's mushroom, big, gray, half-eaten, and surrounded by boar droppings; and *poganka*, which means poisonous fungus and also to heap hurtful words upon someone.

Then the sky blues. A breeze begins to drop acorns through layers of yellow leaves and sun. Stopping by a set of thermometers that poke from the moss like pale buds, Ilya Osipov describes the ecological monitoring that is the heart of the zapovedniki system.

Swaths of cleared land exactly one kilometer (about two-thirds of a mile) apart form a grid throughout Priٰoksko-Terrasnyy. The entire staff periodically makes a sweep of these lines to count animal tracks and droppings. Within each distinct type of habitat, a grid of finer scale is marked off across 25 hectares (a hectare being 2.5 acres) for small mammal counts, detailed bird observations, and vegetation maps. Then, within that grid, one typical hectare is singled out for still more intensive sampling.

Ilya studies wood-eating insects. From the type and number of holes chewed in a given part of the trunk, he can gauge almost precisely how close a tree is to the end of its life span. Among the experts he consults are five species of tiny bark beetles in the family *Scolytidae*. "Somehow," he says, "they can smell the difference in chemical composition when a tree begins to weaken, either from old age or a change in the environment. That's when they attack. For all our elaborate instruments and measuring techniques, we can't tell as much about the condition of a tree as these insects can."

Leah Bendavid-Val, National Geographic Staff

Asian lotuses spread ten-inch pink blossoms on the Volga Delta at Astrakhan'. At this, their northernmost point, warm summers encourage luxuriant growth, particularly in sluggish inlets called *kultuk.* One theory holds that their seeds were borne this far north in the droppings of migrant birds; another, that Buddhist settlers brought the plants here in the 17th century.

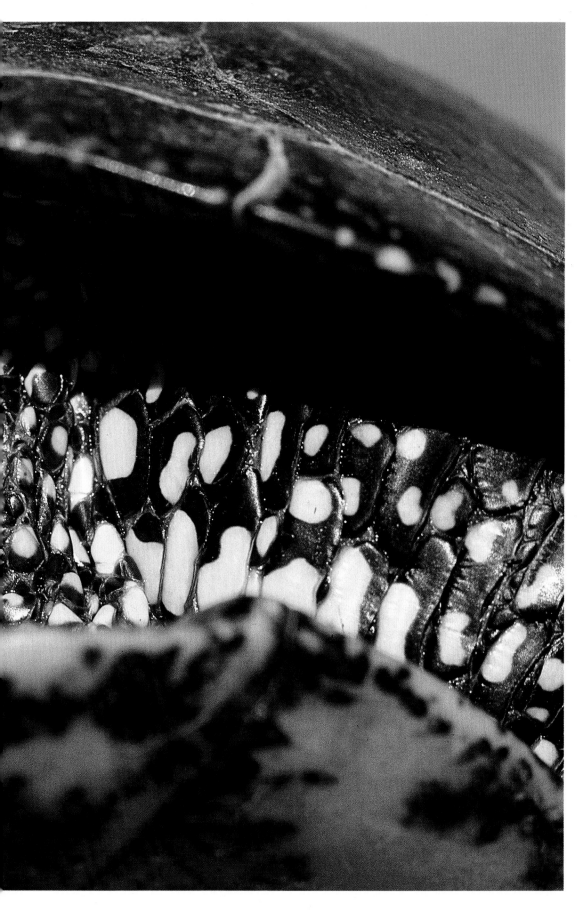

A European pond turtle is caught by the camera before it can dive for cover on the river bottom. These skittish creatures shy from the slightest disturbance. Found farther north than any other turtle, European pond turtles range up to about a foot in length. They line the banks at Astrakhan' in company with countless snakes and frogs—the latter sometimes serving as turtle dinner.

Snarled in a net, a bearded reedling (opposite) awaits rescue by one of the Astrakhan' ornithologists who set the net (below). The reed-dwelling species finds a rich diet of insects in its sheltered habitat. Once tagged with a leg band, the bird will add data to behavior studies at the Caspian Ornithological Station run by the park.

Another researcher at the reserve keeps track of holes made by woodpeckers preying on beetles. Another examines the rate at which leaves, nests, and insect remains fall from the forest canopy to build up soil. Still others focus on soil microorganisms, or soil chemistry, or subsurface water. Moreover, since Priosko-Terrasnyy was added to the list of biosphere reserves in 1978, its primary weather station has been expanded to record such environmental factors as acid rain and airborne heavy metals.

Think of every possible way you can ask a forest questions. That's essentially what the staff at Priosko-Terrasnyy is up to. Work of this sort has countless practical applications for forests used to produce timber and other resources, just as findings from other reserves can prove invaluable to agriculture, fisheries, and game management. The complex monitoring data are summarized in an annual publication entitled *Chronicles of Nature*. As with migrating birds, the legacy of understanding being built reaches well beyond the U.S.S.R.'s borders.

Priosko-Terrasnyy has one more vital function: It is a center for the breeding and restoration of the wisent, or European bison. On nearly 500 acres divided into corrals live 50 to 75 captive bison and their offspring. When the youngsters approach one year of age, they are placed with other yearlings and two-year-olds and allowed to wander through the reserve and surrounding areas, adjusting to more natural conditions. However, regular feeding at troughs ensures that they don't stray too far for too long. It also makes it easier for the staff to capture a few from time to time and ship them off "to the wild life" in Soviet forests within the species' former range.

Bison bonasus is more slender than the *Amerikanski Bison bison* and far less sociable, preferring to roam woodlands in small family groups. Watching wisents up close as they banged bearded heads in dominance struggles, nuzzled their young, or

reached for a mouthful of oak leaves overhead, I realized how perfectly they had been rendered in Paleolithic cave paintings. Eye-to-eye, these beasts can suddenly transport us to a time when the world bulked and bellowed with the like of mammoths. And as a shaggy, humped bridge to the mind of our ancestors, they provide still another reason for us to preserve endangered species.

Europe's bison were felled along with its forests. They were already scarce by the 16th century. Royal preserves offered some sanctuary from hunters and poachers but not, in the end, from soldiers. Troops shot and ate most of the wild bison in the Białowieża Forest on the Polish-Russian border during the First World War, and a poacher killed the last one in 1919. Many of the wild bison hanging on in the Caucasus Mountains were shot during the chaos of the 1918-1920 civil war in the Soviet Union; by 1927 they were all dead.

That left the world with exactly 48

European bison, all in zoos or private parks. Those have since been multiplied into 23 free-roaming populations—4 in Poland and 19 in the Soviet Union. Prioksko-Terrasnyy, under the leadership of Mikhail Zablotsky, has contributed the greatest share of seed stock—210 animals.

Zablotsky, now 74, arrives for dinner at the guest cabin in a suit breasted with medals from the Second World War. A stuffed bear named Misha stands at the head of the table eyeing our plates and vodka glasses while Zablotsky tells a tale of the bull Kavkaz, who, captured in the Caucasus in 1907, was the sole bison from his mountain subspecies to reproduce in captivity. Bred to females of the Białowieża subspecies, he generated the Caucasian-Białowieża line that now populates forests in the Caucasus and Carpathian Mountains.

Sometime in the hours after midnight, Zablotsky rises, gathers his scientific papers—representing 51 years of research and hope for the salvation of a life-form—and bids all a good-night. Upon turning to leave, his gaze falls upon some old photographs of bison on the wall. He must have seen these pictures countless times. But from the softness in his pale blue eyes, you might think he had just discovered the portrait of some family member. "My beloved animals," he whispers, then straightens his shoulders and walks away to bed.

Three weeks later, a bison band grazes in a meadow below me within sight of Mount Pshekish, where Kavkaz was captured as a calf. These days, the Caucasus range harbors well over a thousand bison. Most of them dwell in the 1,017-square-mile Kavkaz reserve, established in 1924 and made a biosphere reserve in 1978. Its present staff includes 45 scientific workers. And this is only one of 34 state nature reserves in the Caucasus region.

Whereas the Caspian Sea, at the eastern end of the Caucasus, actually lies 90 feet below sea level, several peaks in the main

Caucasus range exceed 16,500 feet in height. Given the array of altitudes and climates, the Caucasus can claim the most varied collection of native plants in Europe—some 6,000 species. The tallest peak in Kavkaz reserve, on the range's western end, is 11,023 feet, while a separate section of the reserve extends down to 650 feet—practically to the edge of the Black Sea.

Legends have Jason and the Argonauts passing through the Dardanelles and up the Black Sea coastline in their search for the Golden Fleece. What they found instead were subtropical forests several million years old that include evergreen ancestors of modern deciduous plants, says botanist Mikhail Pridnya, Kavkaz's chief scientist. He is leaning against a vine-tressed female yew tree, itself more than a thousand years old; three men with linked arms couldn't begin to enclose the matriarch's trunk.

As at Astrakhan' and Prioksko-Terrasnyy, Kavkaz reserve maintains a museum open

A bison bull (opposite) nuzzles a female at Prioksko-Terrasnyy reserve, where a breeding program has helped reclaim the European bison from near extinction. The young are raised in a nursery area, then set loose in the reserve. At about two years of age, some are shipped off to roam free in Soviet mountain forests. Lured into a pen with grain, each youngster is coaxed into a box and transported by truck to its new home.

to all. "We consider it our duty to educate the public, or else our work in conservation will be for naught," Mikhail tells me. Like many zapovedniki personnel, he produces brochures and popular articles as well as technical reports. He lectures at schools and to citizen groups, and tours foreign scientists through the reserve. Kavkaz staff are also training guides for 734-square-mile Sochi National Park, recently set in place between the reserve and the crowded, sun-lotion-scented resorts of the coast.

Back in the high country, mammalogist Anatoliy Kudakhtin leads the way past giant beech, oak, and fir. The underbrush roars with Caucasian red deer stags in the rutting season. We pass on into alpine meadows and keep scrambling straight up. With more and more bright peaks coming into view around us, I suddenly realize that I had completely forgotten which nation I was in. I just knew I was in fine country, and that, whether they are Eastern bloc or Western, capitalist or Communist, people who set aside reserves to protect such country and its wild lives aren't preparing to blow up the future. They are making a commitment to save it.

Furry-faced, tireless, curious about everything and given to growling with glee over his dinner, Anatoliy—Tolya—reminds me of several mountain folk and a couple of different grizzlies that I know in Montana. At last we drop our packs to peer through the chink in a knife-edge ridge. Crossing a snowfield on the lee side are tracks of a European brown bear, headed for some lode of ripe chestnuts lower down.

Occasionally, Tolya says, a wild boar will drive a wild bear from its feeding spot. A big, tusky male pig may even follow a wolf pack around and argue about leftovers. Just under a dozen wolf families dwell in the reserve. Tolya has kept track of them for 15 years by foot and cross-country ski, surviving rides in three avalanches. He is addicted to wolves and bears. It's their intelligence

A herd of wild bison thunders along an alpine lake in Kavkaz reserve, which contains a bison population of more than 1,000. Unlike the pure-blooded European bison (above) being released from Priaksko-Terrasnyy, Kavkaz herds present an anomaly: Because of crossbreeding experiments at the beginning of the 20th century, they share the blood of the hardy American bison.

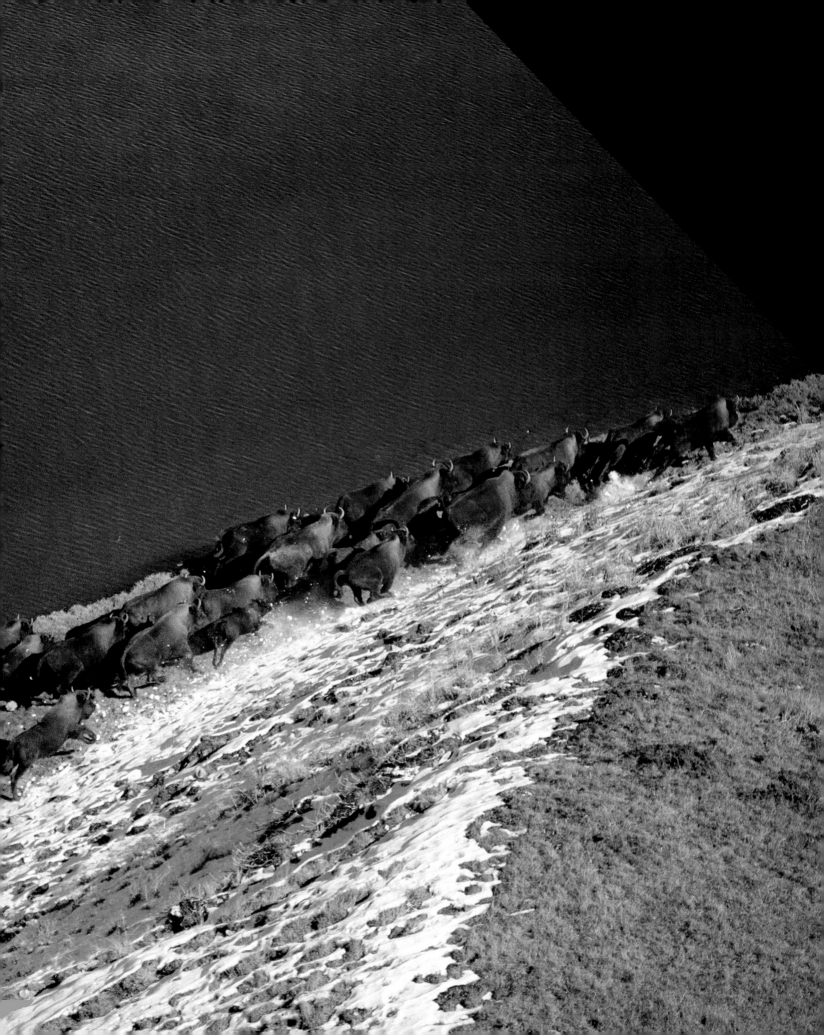

Eroded, glacier-scoured crags form typical terrain at Kavkaz's higher altitudes, while alpine meadows (above) spangle mountain flanks with vivid wildflowers. With environments ranging from 11,000-foot mountain peaks down to the Black Sea coast, Kavkaz has an extraordinary variety of plant and animal life. Some 20 percent of its 1,500 plant species grow only here.

and individuality, he insists; they've spoiled him for studying hoofed herd-dwellers, such as the chamois and Caucasian ibex watching us climb. But he is eager to know more about the three kinds of felines here: small forest cat, lynx, and the rare leopard.

"This is my work; this is my hobby," grins the man-bear. His only regret is that Kavkaz, large as it is, is not larger. Its boundaries reflect human history more than the needs of wide-ranging animals. This is a problem at Astrakhan', where wolves are killed when they become too dense, and at Prioksko-Terrasnyy, where boars must be shot in the absence of wolves. In fact, it is a universal problem for parks and reserves. The U.S.S.R. is working toward expanding its reserves to reflect ecological boundaries.

Kavkaz reserve's bison embody the problems of human influence. Earlier in the century, when it looked as though extinction was at hand, some Caucasian bison were bred to captive New World bison. So while other parts of the region wound up with Caucasian-Białowieża descendants of the bull Kavkaz, the herds found in Kavkaz reserve today are Caucasian-Białowieża-American crosses whose future is puzzled over by Soviet experts. Should the hybrids be blotted out? Kept isolated forever? Soviet biologists fear the hybrids will inevitably contact one day the pure-blooded European bison they fought so hard to reestablish.

We can learn to do better. That's what zapovedniki are for. For seeing how nature works—in a microscopic parasite or the sweep of a bear-tracked meadow on top of the world—and for sharing that knowledge across national boundaries. At Astrakhan' reserve, German Rusanov put it this way: "We come from different countries with different political philosophies. But we have one and the same mother."

You know her name. Nature, the original superpower, is the mother of us all.

**By Douglas H. Chadwick
Photographs by Art Wolfe**

Latin America

The *autocarril,* a diesel bus modified to run on tracks, departs the old Inca city of Quito before first light. The Andean air is thin and cold. By dawn the bus is winding through the high grassland called paramo, under the 19,000-foot, snowcapped dome of the volcano Cotopaxi. At midday the bus comes to the verge of the Andes and plunges down the western side; by afternoon it is chugging through heat and humidity across Ecuador's flooded coastal plain. This seems not just another terrain, but another world.

The iron rails of the autocarril make just one slice through Latin America, the most diverse of places: a land of high cordilleras and steamy coastal plains, fiords and pampas, volcanoes and glaciers, puna and *pantanal,* wet cloud forests and the driest desert on earth. In highland Ecuador, Cotopaxi National Park preserves a surviving piece of Ecuadorian dry forest, along with its great Andean volcano. In Peru, the Pampa Galeras National Reserve safeguards vicuñas, endangered cousins of the camel; Paracas National Reserve protects a portion of the Pacific coastal desert and the adjoining ocean; Lachay National Reserve protects, among other things, wild relatives of the tomato. (Should some catsup crisis—some worldwide tomato blight—require an infusion of genes from the wild, then the world will turn to Lachay.)

In Colombia, Salamanca Island National Park preserves mangroves. In Costa Rica—a small country committed to tropical research—Monteverde Cloud Forest Reserve protects cloud forest, and Guanacaste National Park conserves dry tropical forest.

The greatest wilderness of Latin America, the heart of biological diversity, is in the great rain forest of the Amazon basin, a many-layered green canopy stretching 2,000 miles from the Andes to the Atlantic. It is a forest of dizzying heterogeny. A hundred species of trees may grow on a given acre. For a botanist on foot, it is often half an hour's task to find two trees of the same type. That ground-floor diversity is compounded

Argentina and Brazil

Iguazú National Park
Iguaçu National Park

With a ground-shuddering roar, the Iguaçu River thunders over a two-mile-wide crescent of lava linking Argentina and Brazil. The world's widest waterfall sends up a perpetual cloud of mist, prompting local Guaraní Indians to call it "the place where clouds are born." Daredevil swifts nest on narrow ledges behind the curtain of falling water. National parks at each end of the falls preserve 925 square miles of subtropical rain forest tangled with palms, bamboos, vines, and jewel-toned flowers. Through the gray-green forest flit more than 20 species of butterflies in every color of the rainbow.

as the forest rises through its successive canopies, for each tree is host to dozens of bromeliads, orchids, lichens, liverworts, frogs, lizards, insects, and birds. It is a deep and unplumbed gene pool. It is one of the last great wildernesses in which a human can truly lose himself. It is an enduring mystery. Thousands of rain forest plant species remain undescribed by science, and *millions* of insect species. Countless cures and revelations await us in the dimness of the understory and in the brilliant sunlight among the crowns. Of all plants known to be useful against cancer, 70 percent grow in the tropical forest, yet less than one percent have been chemically analyzed.

In Brazil, where most of Amazonia lies, 29 national parks and 15 biological reserves have been declared. Through the 1960s the aim of Brazilian park planners was to preserve scenic beauty; since the mid-1970s, the emphasis has shifted to preserving ecosystems. How big must a rain forest preserve be, biologists ask, in order to make ecological sense? How important are Pleistocene refugia to the dynamic of the forest?

These refugia are a new discovery: forests within the forest that until 20 years ago we failed to see for the trees. The German geologist Jürgen Haffer identified a dozen places of high endemism and rich species diversity. He suggested that in the dryness and cool of the ice ages, these had been islands of forest in the savanna, refuges from which the Amazon basin was recolonized when the globe warmed up once more.

An artificial ice age has descended on Amazonia, and savannas are spreading there again. The agency is not the ice this time, but *Homo sapiens*. Tropical forest is disappearing faster than a major ecosystem has ever disappeared. An area the size of England, Scotland, and Wales combined—50 million acres of tropical forest—is lost or degraded each year. Parks are vital to all plans to slow or halt this decline. With the chill expansion of humanity across the face of the earth, the refugia need to be pressed into service.

Guatemala

Tikal National Park

Gleaming white in the sunshine, pre-Columbian pyramids tower above a sea of tropical green in enduring testimony to the genius of the ancient Maya. Here, deep in the Petén jungle of northern Guatemala, the Maya built one of their fabled capitals. Settled around 600 B.C., Tikal flourished between the third and eighth centuries A.D. As many as 40,000 people may have lived in the 50-square-mile city. Then, abruptly and for reasons still unknown, the Maya abandoned Tikal around A.D. 900. Its palaces and ball courts, covered marketplace and broad causeways fell silent.

Today the unspoiled rain forest is a 230-square-mile sanctuary for an array of jungle creatures. Jaguars, now endangered but once revered by Maya royalty, still lurk in the undergrowth. The raucous squawks of parrots and the rustling of monkeys break the stillness, and wild turkeys sometimes race across the Great Plaza.

Ecuador

Galápagos National Park

The only oceangoing lizards, marine iguanas of the Galápagos sneeze showers of excess brine absorbed from seawater. A hawk touches down on a giant tortoise (below), a goliath weighing up to 600 pounds.

A natural laboratory of evolution, these volcanic islands were colonized by chance migrants that flew, floated, or swam 600 miles westward from mainland South America. Species evolved in isolation, adapting to the distinctive conditions of each island, from bone-dry Española to lush Santa Cruz. When Charles Darwin visited the Galápagos in 1835, he noted variations in animals that led to his theory of evolution by natural selection.

No longer isolated, this fragile island ecosystem and its unique wildlife are protected by a 3,000-square-mile national park surrounded by a 27,000-square-mile marine reserve.

S. Pölking, Bildagentur Mauritius

Argentina

Los Glaciares National Park

Creaking, popping, and groaning, Moreno Glacier creeps 33 miles down an Andean mountainside into Lake Argentino. House-size chunks of ice break loose and crash into the water, floating away as icebergs.

Eight other major glaciers flow into Los Glaciares National Park from the southern Patagonian ice field, the largest sheet of ice in the Southern Hemisphere outside Antarctica. The park is ravaged by some of the harshest weather on earth. Storms dump rain, sleet, and snow, and 125-mile-an-hour winds scour trenches in the ice.

Despite the frigid conditions, wildlife abounds. Hare-size pudu, the world's smallest deer, live in forested valleys in the foothills. Hummingbirds flash among beech trees. Even at high altitudes, reddish green parakeets fly over ice tinted watermelon pink by algae that feed on nutrients in the snow.

Chile

**Torres del Paine
National Park**

Near the southern reaches of
the Andes, the glaciated peaks
of the Torres del Paine range
climb as high as 8,530 feet.
Thrust aloft by the collision of
gigantic tectonic plates, the
park's namesake *torres,* or
towers, have been rising for at
least 65 million years. These
rugged granite peaks, sheer
and remote, remained un-
climbed until the late 1950s.

Condors and eagles skim
the mountain ridges, while wild
guanacos (below) graze in valley meadows. Once hunted
by Patagonian Indians for food
and fur, these 250-pound
cousins of the llama find refuge
today in this remote corner of
southern Chile.

Günter Ziesler

A capuchin monkey eats a palm stem plucked from the lush rain forest of Manú. Largely undisturbed by humans, the reserve protects the richest diversity of plant and animal life in Amazonia.

Travels in the Rain Forest

I stood at the hotel counter in Lima.

"Where are you going?" the clerk asked.

"Manú."

"Where?"

"A rain forest. It's a park, in the Amazon."

"Oh." She shuddered, and looked back at her paper.

It was late September, and spring was turning to summer in Peru. The rainy season would soon begin. In a few days I was riding in a jeep through the countryside with photographer Bill Curtsinger and a Peruvian crew. We left the paved road and climbed higher into the Andes. There were adobe houses, eucalyptus trees, cactuses, horses, sheep, and llamas. We came to Paucartambo, by a rushing stream, and in the plaza where the old men sat, we could have been in Spain.

The desert began to turn green. There was moisture in the air. A small green house appeared, and a sign on it read Parque Nacional del Manú, 3,500 meters.

Manú National Park, about 6,000 square miles, was created by government decree in 1973; four years later, another 1,000 square miles were added to the park and the whole area declared the Manú Biosphere Reserve, more than 7,000 square miles stretching from the Andes deep into the Amazon. The biosphere reserve, almost half the size of Switzerland, is a fully contained life system, comprising a community of humans, plants, and animals.

We were on the eastern edge of the Andes, at the southern edge of the biosphere reserve, which was divided into three zones. There was the cultural zone (353 square miles), where people could live and farm, bordered by the Alto Madre de Dios River; the reserved zone (992 square miles), open for tourism and scientific research; then the park, most of which lay unexplored, and closed to the outside world.

We camped at a lookout called Tres Cru-

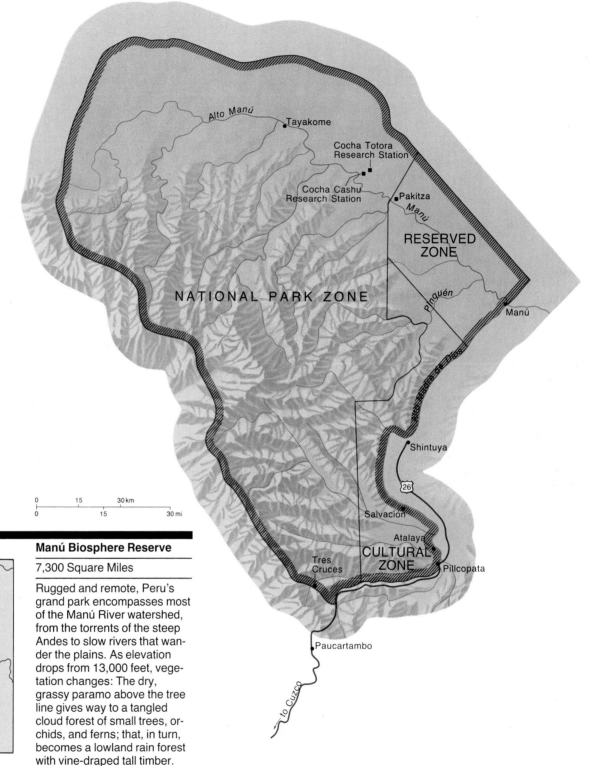

Alto Manú
Tayakome
Cocha Totora
Research Station
Cocha Cashu
Research Station
Pakitza
Manú

RESERVED
ZONE

NATIONAL PARK ZONE

Pinguén

Manú

Shintuya

26

Salvación
Atalaya
CULTURAL
ZONE
Tres
Cruces
Pillcopata

Paucartambo

to Cuzco

0   15   30 km
0   15   30 mi

Manú Biosphere Reserve

7,300 Square Miles

Rugged and remote, Peru's grand park encompasses most of the Manú River watershed, from the torrents of the steep Andes to slow rivers that wander the plains. As elevation drops from 13,000 feet, vegetation changes: The dry, grassy paramo above the tree line gives way to a tangled cloud forest of small trees, orchids, and ferns; that, in turn, becomes a lowland rain forest with vine-draped tall timber. Warm temperatures and ample moisture—some 80 inches of rain annually—provide a year-round growing season.

ANDES MOUNTAINS

Manú
Biosphere
Reserve

PERU

Lima

Cuzco

Pacific
Ocean

ces. Behind us, on a burned-over prairie, a few cattle grazed. Night came and with it flashes of lightning, a few at first, and then giant wishbones and long horizontal lines lit up the sky. It was blinding and came unceasingly, like waves in the ocean. At dawn the sun rose behind clouds, and we descended by the road through elfin forest and masses of lichen. The air was warm, almost balmy. There was the smell of myrtles. Birds called. The wind flowed by. It was a Mediterranean morning. We pulled over as a truck, filled with aguano wood and sleeping workers, strained up the hill.

We bounced down the dirt road, the air grew thicker, the foliage greener. We sweated in the heat. There were wide clearings and burned fields with many tree stumps. We came to a place called Pillcopata, of wood-plank shacks, rusting trucks, beer signs, and naked children. An old man watched us out of the side of his eyes; a woman with a twisted face laughed in the heat. By late afternoon we reached Atalaya. A man slept in a hammock, another sat in the shade with a beer; a woman in tight red pants and black high heels smiled as she peeled an avocado with a long shiny knife. Here the road ended for us.

We swatted flies and loaded our gear into a 30-foot canoe with an Evinrude 55 in the back. The Alto Madre de Dios flowed by, gray-brown and 150 yards wide. It would take us to the Manú River, into the park.

Gustavo Moscoso, a strong young man in shorts and a T-shirt, came over. His bare feet sank in the mud. Mosquitoes homed in.

"*Vámonos.*" Gustavo grinned.

"*Sí,*" I said. "Let's go."

We raced through the rapids and the smooth-flowing water. The air rushed by and we bathed in its coolness. Darkness fell. We pushed on. Finally we pulled over on a sandbar and camped in a clearing among three palm houses where Gustavo, his father, and five brothers lived. The crickets and cicadas lulled us to sleep.

The next day we continued on. One of Gustavo's brothers, Darwin, had joined us, and he sat at the bow, watching for logs. The jungle was thick on either side. Occasionally there was a clearing, a palm-roof house and a red clay bank. Our guide, David Ricalde Ríos, sat on a gunwale, pointing out birds. "Those are black vultures, that is a great black hawk, blue-and-yellow macaws, a large-billed tern, a horned screamer, scarlet macaws." I swung my binoculars around, trying to keep up. More birds live in South America than in any other continent, and more in Peru than any country. Manú has perhaps a thousand bird species, more than most countries have.

David pointed northeast. "Over that mountain range is Paititi, lost city of the Incas. When the Incas fled the Spaniards, they took their best gold and escaped to the jungle. Maybe it's true. Adventurers have tried to find it." He put his toothbrush into the water. Bill looked at me, and we stared

at the mountains in the distance.

"Cloud cover has prevented satellite photography," a Peruvian woman had told me earlier. "The ancient gods protect the city." I remembered how her eyes had lit up.

David watched us, his mouth white with toothpaste. "It would be very difficult to get in there."

We reached the Manú River and turned northwest, upstream. On one bank a small group of naked women bathed in the water. Their faces were wide and pale, their black hair long and cut straight across their foreheads. White strings of beads went from their ears to their noses. We stared at one another, and their eyes seemed far away.

"Yaminahua," said David quietly. Across the river two men poled a dugout canoe while a third man sat between them. One put a finger in his mouth and pulled hard against his cheek.

"Maybe he's sick," said David.

"I think he wants to talk," said Bill.

"Maybe he wants us to come over," I said.

"We cannot stop," said David. "We do not want to see them again. They steal, they touch everything, they are curious." He was quiet, nervous for the first time.

For years these Indians lived deep in the forest. They sang many songs. They even had a song to stop the rain. Then, in 1984, they made their first contact with outsiders, attacking a group of woodcutters in their territory. The Indians were captured and taken to Sepahua, a mission station. When they returned to the forest, they carried diseases for which they had no immunity—whooping cough, malaria, and pneumonia. More than 150 died as a result of that contact, at least half of their population. The people move every six months. No one knows why. Perhaps it is because a great evil has befallen them, and they are afraid.

We moved on. Driftwood appeared, giant stacks of it, like crushed sailing ships along the river. Manú is one of the few places in the Amazon basin where natural stands of mahogany and tropical cedar still grow. Everywhere else they have been cut down. Manú has been preserved because for centuries it was too difficult to reach. Now 300 tourists visit a year. Each pays a small entrance fee.

We saw two giant rodents the size of sheep scrambling up the bank; a collared peccary, a kind of wild pig, swam across, pumping its legs like a dog, its snout above water and surrounded by flies; large black spider monkeys stared at us from tall trees.

We entered the forest, and it was cooler beneath its canopy and not as dense as it looked from the river. I had expected more animals, snakes hanging from trees, parrots and long-billed birds calling from above. We followed a trail cut for scientists and tourists, but we could have made our way without a machete. I had thought we would have to hack our way through. The forest was dry, and leaves cracked beneath our feet. The rains must come soon. David pointed to a tree. A dozen squirrel monkeys, light brown and a foot long, jumped nimbly from vine to vine, foraging for fruit. They could travel several miles looking for food this way; if there was no fruit, the monkeys would eat insects. The monkeys moved on and the forest was quiet.

We camped on a beach called Salvador. Bill eyed the cool water. "I saw a movie of piranhas devouring a cow to the bone," he said. He swatted the bugs around his head in vain, slapped his arms. Darwin smiled, took off his shirt, and waded out into the river. "It is better to splash to keep the stingrays away," he said as he dived in. He came up. "Piranhas? No problem." He laughed.

I waded in and we swam against the current, barely keeping even with the land.

The next morning Darwin took over for Gustavo and carefully read the river, avoiding sandbars and submerged logs. Benito Baca, our cook, read a biology book. David and Bill scanned the forest with binoculars.

The next day, we passed from the reserved zone into the park—seven days out of Lima. An anhinga dived from a branch into the water, stuck its long thin neck up, looked around, and went under again, hunting for fish. A jabiru, a magnificent giant stork, stood alone on a sandbar. I felt a sharp pain between my toes. I took off my shoe and pulled out a tick.

Ten miles inside the park we reached Cocha Totora, one of two scientific stations. It and Cocha Cashu, the larger station, with 21 scientists, less than a mile away, would be home for the next few weeks. At Cocha Totora there was a cedar house, with a palm roof and screen siding, which stood off the ground. We camped nearby.

That night it rained, pouring powerful sheets of water. Sometime before dawn it let up, and I woke to a strange sound, like wind rushing through a giant tunnel. Where was I? It stopped and I dozed off. Later I crawled from my tent and the forest had changed. It was a bright emerald green. The air was fresh and sweet. Water still fell from leaves and vines. Fungi, mushrooms, and bamboo had sprung up overnight, it seemed. A young snake, skinny as my finger, translucent, blue-green and yellow, raised its head six inches from the leaves; birds sang, more it seemed, than before.

"Howler monkeys," said David, as we sipped coffee. It was their roaring cry that had wakened me earlier. David's eyes, trained by passion, knew every bird and animal in the forest. At night he sometimes lay awake practicing their calls. He, like others in Manú, was possessed with a sense of urgency. Only 5 to 10 percent of the rain forest's flora and fauna have been identified. More than a fourth of our medicines contain extracts from tropical plants; only one percent of plants have been screened for value. The forest, like oil, is a finite resource.

The sun rose over Cocha Totora, an oxbow lake 180 yards wide and 1,000 yards long. Three dugout canoes lay tied to trees in the still water. Benito strummed a guitar.

He had made pancakes in a frying pan on the cabin's old kerosene stove. Darwin read a Western, Bill prepared his cameras. It rained almost every day now, sometimes pouring for hours, hatching more mosquito larvae. We stalked the jungle, gradually learning to see and smell and hear. We went to a salt lick to wait for the parrots and macaws to feed on the minerals. It rained for three days, Bill sweated in his blind, and we waved the mosquitoes away from our soup. A hundred parrots and macaws waited in the trees but did not come down. Big chunks of riverbank crashed into the water. The Manú River was rising.

"Fish will now have more food," David explained. "Many of them have developed stronger teeth to chew fruits and seeds. They leave seeds along the riverbanks, which become beaches as the river moves, and new trees will grow."

John Terborgh, professor of biology at Princeton University, has been studying Manú since 1973. He is adviser to a family of young scientists at Cocha Cashu. We sat in the hut that was his kitchen and dining hall. He finished a plate of rice and lentils, and poured black coffee from a thermos. Why, I asked, did it rain so much?

He picked up an onion. "The Earth is like a round ball and at the Equator is perpendicular to the sun. More sunlight impinges on the equatorial zone than anywhere else; it hits the center directly. It takes energy to evaporate water, and this tremendous energy from the sun evaporates the moisture in the jungle. What goes up must come down. Precipitation is slight at the Earth's poles. Water is also transported in air masses west from the Atlantic, with the prevailing winds, until it hits the Andes. Most of our moisture comes from evaporation from the forests. This is why vegetation is so important. If we cut down the forest, we drastically reduce the rainfall."

A few days later we took a path north, one of many the scientists had cut through their

laboratory. We crossed through the underbrush to a small channel, and sank to our knees in mud. David whistled for Benito, who finally responded, waiting where he had captured two caimans the night before.

"I shined a flashlight in his eyes, blinded him, then went into the water. I found out where his head and tail were, mounted him from behind, wrapped my belt around him, grabbed the tree, and brought him to shore." Benito, with a degree in biology from Cuzco University, was a specialist on the crocodile relative that grows to 15 feet.

Wasn't he afraid?

He shrugged and waded in his rubber boots and old khaki clothes toward the five-foot-long reptile tied to the tree. The caiman hissed deeply, like a dragon. A baby caiman lay tied in the water 20 feet away. Benito left the adult and waded over to the baby. He picked it up behind the head.

"It was fast, like catching a cat," he said. He examined it, cut a scale from its tail to mark the animal, then kissed it on its head and, pointing like a father, watched it swim away. We stood quietly in the mud as Benito approached the other reptile. It hissed again. Slowly, Benito took a 12-foot aluminum pole and placed the lasso at one end around the caiman's neck. The caiman lashed out. Slowly, with a white cord, Benito wrapped the animal's jaws shut.

Above, Lawrence's thrush mimicked the calls of other birds in the forest.

Benito dragged the caiman, now subdued, over to a log and measured it. Benito grinned, his gold tooth prominent, and clenched his fists. "I felt this species was here, but they said I was crazy."

The caiman lashed out, broke the noose, and twisted away. Benito waded after it, up to his stomach, then his chest. Minutes passed. We were silent. The caiman would starve with its jaws tied shut. Benito ducked under by a fallen tree and emerged, dragging the reptile by the tail. Gently, he cut the cord and the caiman slid away.

"I learned about techniques from books," Benito said. "I love my work, and I feel it is important. Someday I would like to manage caimans." The water was dark.

Fernando Cornejo, a forester studying at Cocha Cashu, carried a chart in his hand, a tape measure around his neck, and a pencil in his ear. His shirt was torn. "What interests me," said Fernando, "is the relationship between the forest and the animals in it." He picked up a small piece of fruit.

He pointed to a tree. "This is a *Pseudolmedia*. Spider monkeys, capuchins, and curassows only eat the fruit's pulp and drop the seeds as they travel through the canopy. See how this tree has too much latex in its bark for termites. Vines will not strangle it."

We came to a ficus tree, a hundred feet long, lying in our path. Its roots were less than a yard long. "The oldest tree in the jungle is probably 300 years old," said Fernando. "The most valuable species are slow growing. We need fast-growing trees for the money they can generate; no one has the patience to wait 200 years for a mahogany."

Rolando Gutierrez, another scientist, came over, parting his way with a black-handled machete. He carried a blowgun and darts for tagging birds. "The richness of the tropical forest is in the canopy above us, not in the soil," he said. "As leaves fall, their nutrients stay on the ground. Other plants retain them and use those nutrients to grow. It is like a net. When the river passed through here, bringing its rich nutrients, the species started. Energy comes from the sun and the river."

Night was falling. I had to return to camp. Hours later I flashed the light on the leaves outside my tent. It was 2:45 a.m. I looked at the forest but could not see beyond my hand. At 3 a.m. I would meet Bettina Torres, a scientist working at Cocha Cashu, at the cabin.

"I was scared," she said, describing her first night walk in the forest. "I saw snakes everywhere. I thought of jaguars." Now she

A thick liana vine loops toward the sunlit canopy. The Amazon basin, with its luxuriant growth, provides countless homes for wildlife. One-fifth of all bird species live there, including perhaps a thousand species in Manú alone. Each Manú resident develops a specialty: The tiger heron stalks its prey in shallow pools (above). The crested owl (above left) hunts insects at night.

NEXT PAGES: Macaws, usually seedeaters, nibble clay, perhaps for dietary minerals.
Günter Ziesler

Chip Clark

Clinging to a twig, a katydid mimics a leaf (above) and eludes predators. Other insects rely on a combination of stealth, cooperation, and sheer numbers to survive: Army ants (right) bivouac by day, protecting their young in a blanket of bodies, and march out to hunt by night.

laced up her Vietnam-style combat boots, checked her snakebite kit, compass, writing materials, adjusted her headlamp. "If the lamp goes out, I cannot move a step until dawn." We headed southwest, toward the river. "Walk with your heel first." She exaggerated the step. "That way you won't trip over vines or snakes so easily." She laughed and went ahead.

The jungle was quiet. The air was cool. We walked quickly, maybe out of fear. I flashed my light at vines and sticks, curved and hanging. Bettina stopped. "Smell the garlic. It is a fungus that only lasts one night." It was easier to smell at night.

At the river we saw the sky. Orion was bright and the moon was a crescent. Bettina turned north, then east, stopping to verify her course, or when she heard the curassow call. Birds do not move at night. "If we know its call," she said, "then we can learn where it lives." We crawled over fallen logs, through vines, stopped to listen.

There are more insects out at night and, because of them, more frogs and snakes: bushmasters, fer-de-lance, corals, and others. Ocelots and jaguars came out then too.

At 4:30 a.m. sharp, the male howler monkey began its call. Another answered, and

Charles H. Jason

191

another. They stopped and birds began to sing. The forest awoke. Gradually I could see my hands, the shape of trees and leaves, patches of gray. We came to where a cat had been. The smell of its urine was strong.

Morning was a rich blue-green, and I felt like ancient man. By six we reached Totora. The sun was high, the sky was blue, and soon it was bright and hot.

The next afternoon I heard an alien sound, an outboard motor from far away. A group of people arrived, and the leader, with a bowie knife on his belt, gave me his card. He was the park director. "You may visit Tayakome if you wish," he said. Tayakome was a Machiguenga settlement. The park did not normally allow outside contact with the Indians. No photography allowed, and I could stay only 24 hours.

I signed the letter of permission. We got in the boat and headed upstream, with Darwin as *motorista*. Alejandro de la Cruz Melger, assistant to the director, went with us, and two guides who were Piro Indians.

"I have been to Tayakome before," said Alejandro, "but not beyond. We do not know what is up there." He put his hands in the water, ran them through his hair, put his hat back on.

Small tributaries entered from either side. Our Indian escorts knew the names but not what lay up them.

We came to a clearing with three palm-roof houses and dugout canoes moored to a bamboo pole.

"Machiguenga," said Alejandro. "They engage in commerce with the scientists." He did not seem pleased. The Indians traded avocados, papayas, and limes for batteries, machetes, flashlights, and nylon cord.

At another clearing a man in a madras shirt and green army pants waved for us to stop. Alejandro nodded. Darwin turned the boat. We got out. The man on shore had bright eyes, a chiseled face, and curly black hair. We walked up into the flat, open compound. There were five houses, three on

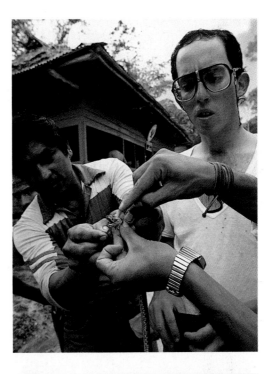

In a laboratory of green, scientists work to uncover the mysteries of the rain forest, where countless plant and animal species await discovery (opposite). Researchers at Pakitza examine a highly poisonous banded snake (right). Near another of Manú's research stations, biologist Benito Baca measures a black caiman (below right) before releasing it. Some unknown species may hold secrets for human survival; a fourth of today's medicines originate in tropical forests.

thick stilts. Inside, bamboo mats were spread across the wood-slat floor.

"His name is Zacharias," said Alejandro, nodding at the Machiguenga Indian who had met us. He was contacted by the Dominicans in 1960 and spoke Spanish. Zacharias offered us watermelon. He had two wives, two teenage girls, a teenage boy. A small boy and girl were naked. The adults, Alejandro said, had dressed for our arrival. There were dogs and parakeets and parrots and other pet birds. There were bugs and mosquitoes and half-eaten fruit. The younger wife had long hair and was pretty, even without her front teeth. The other had close-cropped hair and sat smiling in the house. One wife went into the hut by the fire and sat next to the hollowed-out log in which she made *masato:* manioc plant and saliva, which fermented into beer. We said goodbye. I noticed mosquito nets where the family slept.

At sundown we reached Tayakome, high on a cliff where the river turned sharply east. Twenty men looked down with their arms folded and legs apart. No one smiled. It was quiet. Alejandro and the Piro climbed up to meet them while Darwin and I waited in the boat. Alejandro returned and told Darwin to take the boat north a hundred yards. We moved the boat and hiked up the cliff and camped in a field at the edge of the forest. A man with a straight nose and prominent cheekbones came over. He was Aransabel, a leader. Fourteen families lived in the village. We shook hands.

"We are fine except for problems of territory," the leader said. "The Nahuas." He smiled and shot an imaginary arrow. From the cliff you could see up and down the river. "This is our territory," said Aransabel.

Ten men and women filed past carrying logs on their shoulders. Night fell and Aransabel led us past the huts and down into the forest, where a brook flowed through a gully. There were thin shells of fruit for pouring water and flat pieces of wood on which

Laden with silt from the high Andes, the Pinquén River writhes through Manú's vast lowland tracts. Despite its uniform appearance, the rain forest is really a mosaic of plant communities, some predating the last ice age. Scientists see these unique refuges as vital gene banks.

to sit. I imagined the women bathing here, a young girl combing her mother's long hair. Loud barking sounds came from the forest.

"Kalinowsky's rat," said Darwin, pouring water over himself. "No problem," he said. We went back to our tents. Gray smoke rose from the village and disappeared into the black night, and low voices carried across the field. A child coughed in his sleep.

At dawn we met Aransabel in his hut. Bows and arrows, five feet long, lay across the beams above us. A monkey-skin drum hung from a peg. A fire burned between two logs. A dog slept against one log. One of Aransabel's two wives counted out a stack of palm leaves for cooking bananas and fish.

Do you fish?

"Sometimes we put the barbasco plant in small streams," Aransabel said. "It kills fish. We cook them in smoke."

A small boy went crying to the women. A teenage girl took some fruit and sat on a log by herself. A boy rolled over in a house and coughed violently. I wondered how long he would live.

Do you believe in God?

Aransabel smiled to himself. He too had learned Spanish from the Dominicans. "When we die, we go to the sky to be with God. We bury our dead in the jungle, next to the *catahua* tree. It is the highest, prettiest tree in the forest. We make our canoes and our bows from it."

I asked about fire.

Alejandro said they had matches. Aransa-

bel went to another hut and returned with two pieces of *soga* wood, 18 inches long. It felt and smelled like palm. He placed some hemp on a mat. On top of this he put one of the pieces of wood with a notch in it. He put the other piece of wood upright in the notch and rubbed the wood with his hands. There was dew on the ground, and the air was thick. He worked hard, and finally there was smoke and sparks and a flame in the hemp, and it seemed a miracle.

We walked through the tall grass past a field of manioc plants, past black fields and charred trees and palm-roof houses. At a clearing the hard ground was swept clean, and men and women watched us curiously. A few young men laughed.

I asked about hunting.

"When we hunt," Aransabel said, "the men first sit in a circle and drink masato. It is an ancient ritual. One of our men is hunting now. We need meat for tomorrow. If a man takes too long in the forest, that means he is hunting indiscriminately."

Another man joined us. His name was Mauro. He had thick black eyebrows and was built like a wrestler. He wore jeans and a shirt in the heat.

I asked if he was ever afraid in the forest.

"We never sleep in the forest," Mauro said. "We do not like snakes."

Aransabel spoke again. "We smoke tobacco when we hunt. It keeps snakes away. If someone is bitten, we take the blood of the catahua tree and drink it for one week.

Surveying the world from the edge of a leaf, a tree frog occupies but one niche in the complex web of rain forest life (opposite). In habitats undisturbed for centuries, Manú's wildlife abounds, one species relying on a network of others for survival. Sideneck turtles sun themselves on a log, accompanied by a butterfly (above left); a giant otter snatches a fish from a languid stream (above).

We take little food. If you drink water in that week, it is death. No one dies from snakes."

Mauro spoke. "We hunt monkeys and peccaries, not jaguars or caimans."

A few women in rough hemp dresses watched us. They smiled and did not hide.

I asked about marriage.

"At about nine years one asks for a girl," Mauro explained. "After her first menstruation she can marry. But age is not important. An old woman can marry a young man; an older man can marry a young girl or one the same age. But a man must first show that he can hunt, fish, and farm."

Did they have plants to prevent children, and for abortions, as I had heard?

"Yes," said Mauro, "but the woman must be very careful. If not taken carefully, you die. We have plants for every sickness, except for what comes from outsiders."

Later a young woman brought us watermelon and pineapple. "It is time for these fruits," Mauro said.

Everything in its season. They only hunted what they needed. They did not use salt or sugar. "We do not need anything," Aransabel said. "We are fine."

Our day was up. We loaded the boat and swam in the river with some of the young men. We got out and dried in the sun. The motor kicked in, and up on the cliff the whole village watched us go. I sat in the front of the boat and watched them until we rounded the bend.

It was hot, then it rained fiercely, and afterwards it was hot again. Finally one morning the sky cleared, and we headed out on the river. We stopped near a dugout canoe and hiked to the airstrip. The grass was above our knees, but the Cessna landed safely. We got in, and in a few minutes it rose above the trees and flew along the Manú River, then turned and climbed through the cloud forest and high over the Andes, and then Manú was gone.

By Jere Van Dyk
Photographs by Bill Curtsinger

A sunset haze drifts through the deep valleys of Manú National Park. Such treasures may not last, as the world's tropical forests fall to farmers, loggers, miners, and road builders. With jobs and land scarce, pressure grows for exploitation of the Amazon basin, whose ancient biological bounty can be imperiled in a fraction of the time it took to evolve.

Asia

Before the year 2000, we will have made our final choices in allocating the last of earth's wild lands.

Much of Asia has come to that final choice already. In Indonesia, 175 million people surround a handful of new national parks, the first five of which were dedicated in 1980. In India, parks like Ranthambhore are islands in a sea of 750 million people. In China, parks like Wolong Natural Reserve, with its few dozen pandas, are islands in a sea of a billion people.

India's provision for tomorrow, in the face of the poverty of today, has been remarkable. Gir Forest National Park, a 500-square-mile tract of semiarid woodland dominated by stunted teak, is a refuge for 200 Asiatic lions, the only wild population of *Panthera leo persica* left on earth. The 17 reserves established under India's Project Tiger have sequestered 4,750 square miles that are free from all human use, surrounded by another 5,750 square miles where human activities are controlled. The approach has been to restore the ecosystem, and the tiger is coming back.

At the top of the subcontinent, in the Royal Chitwan National Park of Nepal, park managers are struggling to balance the needs of local people with the needs of tigers, rhinos, and tourists. Resentment of parks by locals is a widespread problem in Asia, given that continent's human numbers and land hunger, and in Chitwan that problem is accentuated by the tendency of the park's tigers and rhinos to kill villagers occasionally. A challenge to Nepalese parks, as to parks everywhere in Asia and the Third World, is to bring more of the park's benefits to the local people. If the locals of Chitwan are not yet convinced of the value of their park, then their high-altitude countrymen, the Sherpas of Nepal's Sagarmatha National Park, are nearly persuaded of the value of their own. The many trekkers who come to Sagarmatha have brought a certain culture shock to the Everest region, but they have also brought money.

For two millennia the wildlife of Sri Lanka has had

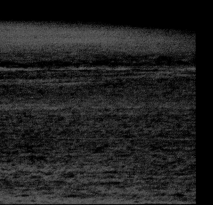

Japan

Ashizuri-Uwakai National Park

Sunset silhouettes the tranquil shores of Ashizuri-Uwakai National Park. The park lies along the southwestern coast of Shikoku, the smallest of Japan's main islands. Cliff-hugging roads offer long, misty views of narrow inlets and islands left by the submergence of mountain valleys. Granite cliffs and natural sandstone sculptures take on fanciful names; Tatsukushi, "dragon skewers," describes one formation that resembles bundles of bamboo stalks.

Below the ocean's surface the warm waters of the Japan Current bathe coral reefs and colorful fish. The marine wonders of the shore at Minokoshi are so numerous that many are bound to be "left unseen," the meaning of the name Minokoshi. And on beaches swept by the *kaiyose,* the seashell-bringing wind, lie countless specimens churned up from the ocean floor. A museum at Tatsukushi devoted entirely to shells displays 50,000 of them.

Cary Wolinsky, Trillium

a measure of protection by Buddhism, and the old Sinhalese kings were given to establishing sanctuaries. (In the 12th century King Nissanka Malla sent out word, by drum, that no animal should be killed within a radius of 7 *gav*—20 miles—of the city of Anuradhapura.) That tradition continues, despite the population's growth to nearly 16 million, and today the island has 9 national parks. In Wilpattu, a tract of more than 500 square miles of jungle on the northwest coast, live crocodiles, sloth bears, spotted deer, elephants, leopards, eagles, and fish owls.

The 1970s saw the greatest expansion of protected areas in world history; the 1990s will see the last.

Perhaps Japan offers a vision of that future, the best we can hope for. The island nation, with 125 million people on a landmass the size of California, has no real wilderness left. (If the traveler in Grand Canyon National Park, which receives 3 million visitors a year, feels crowded, he should consider the traveler in Fuji-Hakone-Izu National Park, which receives 85 million.) Fourteen percent of Japan's land is designated parkland, yet the only land that might be called wild is in Daisetsuzan National Park, on the northernmost island, Hokkaido. The Japanese have made the best of their circumstances, developing a whole aesthetic to accommodate the fix they are in. Shintoism and Buddhism teach followers to see harmony and the macrocosm in a temple garden, in a bonsai tree, in a single leaf. Most of Japan's 27 national parks and its multitude of prefectural parks are small, manicured places.

Japanese parks are lovely, but the synecdochic Japanese view of scenery is worrisome, too, because it is based, in part, on illusion. Nature is not about fragments; it is about wholeness. The bonsai tree is to the natural tree as the toy poodle is to the wolf. The danger, as human numbers swamp the numbers of everything else on earth, is that all mankind will fall, of necessity, into this peculiar derangement, this masterful way of kidding ourselves.

People's Republic of China
Jiuzhaigou National Park

The rough, calcified riverbed at
the crest of Pearl Shoal Waterfall provides sure footing for
the mounts of Tibetan horse-
men. Primitive forest, hillsides
of flowers, a profusion of more
than a hundred lakes, and
countless waterfalls—these
are Jiuzhaigou National Park
in the heart of Sichuan, China's most populous province.
The name of the park means
"nine stockades canyon" because Tibetan villages once
thrived where the panda,
golden-haired monkey, goat-
like takin, and river deer now
live. The valleys are peaceful—valleys like Shuzhengqun-
haigou, where more than 40
shallow lakes and marshes extend for three miles, strung together by waterfalls, bordered
by embankments alive with the
exposed, tangled tree roots
that float in the rushing water.

People's Republic of China

Wolong Natural Reserve

All of eastern China was once the domain of the giant panda; now only a thousand survive, perhaps half of them in such protected environments as Wolong Natural Reserve in Sichuan Province. A cool climate, abundant rainfall, and virgin forests overgrown with bamboo, staple of the panda's diet, make Wolong a haven for the rare creatures—but a haven with a built-in time bomb.

Every hundred years or so, the local bamboo flowers and dies. Once the panda could migrate to new supplies, but now that China's growing population has eliminated extensive bamboo forests, such migrations yield little food. So scientists plan to replant the pandas' favorite bamboo species, and hope to reestablish a habitat destroyed by years of logging and agriculture.

George B. Schaller

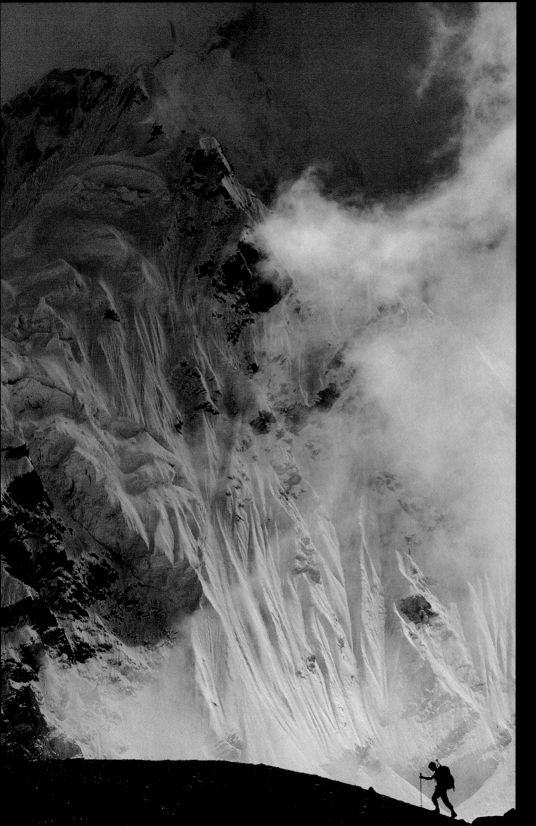

Nepal

Sagarmatha National Park

Sagarmatha is the name given to the highest mountain in the world, the peak "whose head touches the sky." It is also the name of the 450-square-mile national park that surrounds the Himalayan mountain and includes the homes of Nepal's Sherpas, who came from Tibet to settle the area some 400 years ago. The challenge of Sagarmatha, known to many as Mount Everest, and of its neighboring peaks lures climbers and trekkers from all over the world. There are no roads or cars anywhere in the park—those who visit Sagarmatha must cross a swaying foot-bridge to enter. They follow centuries-old Sherpa trails through a land of rhododendrons and birch forests, gla-

Toshinao Kikuchi, World Photo Service

J. & J. Blassi, INCAFO

Philippines

Taal Volcano Island National Park

Taal Volcano stands 40 miles south of Manila on the island of Luzon. Taal's cone emerges from the center of a lake 15 miles wide, formed over 5,000 centuries ago when a volcano erupted and collapsed into a huge caldera. Despite its diminutive size—Taal rises to only 984 feet—it is the most menacing of the Philippines' 14 active volcanoes. Since 1572, over 30 major eruptions have been recorded; the worst occurred in 1911, when no more than 15 of Taal Island's 500 inhabitants survived. Today some 4,000 people live on Taal, their future uncertain.

Taal lies within the domain of the Philippine eagle (above). Fewer than 300 remain, their numbers threatened by hunters and loggers. The eagles' main sanctuary is in Mount Apo National Park on the island of Mindanao.

Sobo-Katamuki
National Park

Deep forests and water-carved rock formations characterize Sobo-Katamuki. Takachiho Gorge, a main feature of the park, figures in the Japanese creation myths, along with Mount Takachiho, 62 miles to the south. From the mountain, so the story goes, fell drops of water from the Heavenly Downward-Pointing Spear, and these became the Japanese islands. Here too, myth says, was born Japan's legendary Emperor Jimmu, a descendant of the sun goddess.

Milan Horacek, Bilderberg Archiv der Fotografen

Japan

Fuji-Hakone-Izu
National Park

"Fuji bare and naked in a blaze of sunshine is beautiful. Fuji with its summit wrapped in cloud and mist is more beautiful; Fuji blotted out by the fog until but a hint or line is left is most beautiful." The words of Frederick Starr, an American anthropologist who climbed Fuji five times, are carved on a monument near the base of the mountain, and they describe Fuji's most irresistible quality—its constantly changing appearance.

Some 500,000 hikers a year ascend Fuji's trails. But the mountain is not the only attraction of Fuji-Hakone-Izu National Park. Sandy beaches, historic towns, and hot springs draw multitudes. So do mountain lakes where visitors fish and swim, skate and boat, and—on a clear day—contemplate the inverted image of the volcanic cone whose name means "everlasting life."

209

Indonesia

Bromo-Tengger-Semeru National Park

Gunung Bromo (Mount Bromo) rises from a sea of gray sand and scrub grass, enclosed within what was once the rim of a much larger volcano in Java's Tengger range. The mountain, stark and forbidding in the midday sun, turns mysterious at dawn when steam and gases from the volcano's cone mix with morning mist. Tenggerese villagers visit the crater to offer food and flowers to the god of the volcano.

A few islands away, in Komodo National Park, lives the Komodo dragon (above). These reptiles, found nowhere else in the world, can grow 10 feet long and weigh 300 pounds. They prey on deer, wild pigs, each other, and, rarely, on humans. Lately some dragons have gotten used to eating goats that tourists offer up to lure the reptiles into view.

211

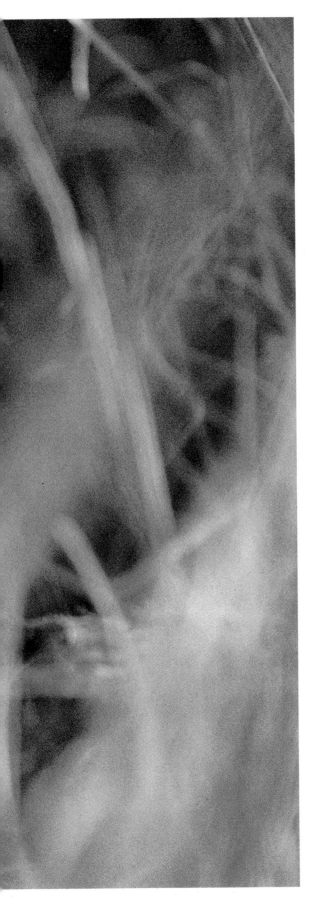

Her muzzle stained with the blood of a slain sambar stag, a feasting Ranthambhore tigress pauses, ever watchful. Tigers number around 40 in the park's forest, almost triple the population existing when Project Tiger was launched in 1973. It set aside several forest reserves to protect tigers, then threatened with extinction.

The Tiger's Fragile Kingdom

There are already three tigers half hidden in the tall yellow grass that surrounds us, a tigress and her two nearly full-grown cubs, when the deep, agitated alarm call of a sambar hind warns of the arrival of still another. Behind us and off to the left, a huge male tiger appears, weighing perhaps 450 pounds, head down and padding steadily toward the open jeep in which my two companions and I are sitting very still.

The tigress sees him coming, too, and sends her male cub bounding away to safety. Then she melts into the grass with her female offspring, away from the sambar carcass that she and her cubs have been eating all morning.

This is my third visit to Ranthambhore National Park, and with me as I watch are Fateh Singh Rathore, the park's former field director, and Valmik Thapar, a bearded young researcher and filmmaker who has devoted much of the past dozen years to Ranthambhore and its tigers.

The big male enters the grass, passing within 20 feet of the jeep and according us a casually malevolent look, then settles down to sleep next to the misappropriated kill.

Everything is quiet for a time, the only sound the buzzing of the flies. Then the tigress reappears, creeping almost imperceptibly through the grass toward the sleeping intruder, precisely the way a kitten might stalk across your living room rug, but on an infinitely more menacing scale. As she places one foot after the other, her eyes never leave the male's back. She comes within ten yards of him, then five feet, then three . . . and touches him with her paw.

The male awakens, roaring. The tigress roars back. The sound seems to split the air. Both animals rear up on their hind legs, massive snarling heads and bared claws high above the grass. They spar for a moment, then, with one blow, the male slaps the much smaller tigress down.

Ranthambhore National Park

150 Square Miles

Once the hunting preserve of the Maharajas of Jaipur, Ranthambhore became a wildlife sanctuary in 1957, a forest reserve in 1973, and a national park in 1981. Deciduous forest and wild savanna change drastically with the seasons. With the monsoons of July, all turns to lush green; by April the landscape is shriveled and scorched. The Indian tiger, along with 300 other animal species, thrives in its natural domain. Liberated from the threat of human hunters and protected by years of enlightened park management, the tigers—once thought to be exclusively nocturnal—have emerged to live and hunt in the daylight. They prowl the forests, lakeshores, and roads, unperturbed even by camera-clicking tourists.

Delhi ★
☐ Ranthambhore National Park
Calcutta •
I N D I A
• Bombay
Indian Ocean

0   2   4 km
0   2   4 mi

Padam Talao   Rajbagh Talao
Ranthambhore Fort   ■ Jogi Mahal Tourist Center
to Sawai Madhopur

She backs off meekly to the shade of the nearest tree to await another chance to feed. Peace returns, broken only by the male's gnawing of sambar bones, the busy flies, the cawing of a far-off jungle crow.

Later, attracted by the sweet, breeze-blown scent of the kill, three wild boars trot toward the grass, then skitter to a stop at its edge as the fainter smell of the tiger reaches them. The anxious pigs skip forward and back, uplifted snouts aquiver, back hair bristling. Hunger and fear compete—tiger kills are free meals for wild boars; wild boars are a favorite tiger food—and fear finally wins out. The pigs wheel and rush off.

"Red-letter day," says Valmik Thapar as he starts the engine and we drive off. "Red-letter day." Even at Ranthambhore, perhaps the most celebrated of India's national parks, to see so much concentrated animal activity so close is a rarity.

Just 15 years ago, such sights would not have been seen at all. The tiger seemed doomed to extinction then: Fewer than 2,000 of these magnificent predators were thought to roam all that was left of Indian jungles, which may have held as many as 40,000 at the turn of the century. Unchecked shooting was partly responsible. In 1970 tiger hunting was banned throughout the country, but the relentless destruction of the tiger's habitat by growing numbers of people and the livestock on which they depended constituted the most serious threat to the survival of the tiger population.

Few countries on earth are beset with more competing problems than is India, and the seriousness with which it has sought to conserve its wildlife is therefore all the more impressive: During the last 15 years the number of national parks and state wildlife sanctuaries has more than doubled, to over 300.

As part of that national effort, Project Tiger was launched in 1973 with help from the World Wildlife Fund. Nine forests were set aside for special protection. Eight have

A tigress in estrus rests briefly in her search for a mate. She prowls the paths of least resistance—Ranthambhore's man-made roads. Tigers also use the park's network of roads to hunt and to patrol their territory, an advantage to park staff who can keep track of their comings and goings by following footprints, or pugmarks.

Günter Ziesler

been added since. Each reserve was to include a sacrosanct core area, off limits to humans, where tigers would be left to live and multiply unmolested. These breeding grounds were to be safeguarded by a broad buffer zone where humans would be allowed only on a severely restricted basis. It was hoped that young tigers would begin to move from each reserve to adjacent forests.

By almost any measure Project Tiger has been a success: The number of tigers, inside and outside the reserves, is believed to have at least doubled, to more than 4,000.

Ranthambhore, the former hunting preserve of the Maharajas of Jaipur, located near the town of Sawai Madhopur in the desert state of Rajasthan, was one of the first nine Project Tiger reserves. Despite the frequent intrusions of poachers and the permanent presence of more than a thousand villagers whose livestock was steadily devouring what was left of the tattered forest, it was still thought to contain 14 tigers.

Ranthambhore would be a spectacular place even if the tiger's roar had never been heard there. Located at the junction of two ranges of red hills, the Vindhyas and Aravallis, it was once the capital of Hindu kings and is still dominated by the domes and sprawling battlements of a hilltop fortress. Strewn throughout its forest are overgrown reminders of the ancient past—crumbling walls, gateways, palaces, and domed chhatris built to mark the site where some prominent man was cremated long ago, now used in winter by tigers seeking the warmth of the early morning sun.

Three lakes, brilliant blue in normal times and filled with lotus plants and the half-submerged sambar that feed on them, run down the center of the park. The broad grassy shores teem with birds and animals—delicate deer called chital, the big ungainly antelope called nilgai, wild boars, marsh crocodiles, white-necked and painted storks, and scores of strutting peacocks. Twenty-two species of mammals have been

Günter Ziesler (left)

January finds the grassy shores of Ranthambhore's lakes teeming with storks and spoonbills, chital and sambar. For sambar, this is the height of the winter rutting season.

Fateh Singh Rathore, Ranthambhore's former field director and ongoing protector, surveys his domain from the park's highest point.

seen in the park—and more than 270 species of birds.

But it is the unusually bold tigers of Ranthambhore that have made it the showpiece of Project Tiger. There are now thought to be upwards of 40 of them within the park's 150 square miles—and the leopards that were once seen with some frequency in its heart have been pushed outward to its rocky fringes by their bigger, more powerful rivals.

Elsewhere in India, visitors hoping to see tigers in the wild must usually content themselves with brilliant flashes of black-and-orange disappearing into dense undergrowth. Here, in this open, unrivaled setting, almost every aspect of their lives lies open to the patient visitor's gaze.

In fact, at Ranthambhore it is easy to lose sight of the fact that while tigers are beautiful, they are never cuddly. I once spent a whole afternoon watching four tigers sleep off a meal, occasionally rolling their full bellies upward, great paws in the air, contented. They were dozing in the shade near a kill; I was sitting in the sun. No human sound disturbed them: Our restless shifting in the jeep had no effect on the steady, bellows-like sound of their breathing; neither did the voices of a road crew in the distance, nor a series of blasts from a rock quarry outside the park. After the third hot, drowsy hour, it was all I could do to keep from getting down to sleep alongside them. Then, the gentle flutter of a tree pie's wings brought the tigress roaring to her feet—and me to my senses. Even the bird's minute threat to her kill had demanded action; so would I have, had I actually got down. But sitting in the jeep, neither menace nor potential meal, I was part of the landscape.

Some Ranthambhore tigers have even learned to exploit the jeeps' loud presence, shrewdly waiting to inch a little closer when the sudden stutter of an engine diverts the nervous quarry's attention. Along with the occupants of half a dozen other vehicles one evening, I watched a tigress take 15 minutes to creep a hundred yards across open ground toward a hillside where she saw a dozen chital. She managed to move so stealthily, despite the lack of cover and the ceaseless clicking of cameras, that she alarmed neither the deer nor the normally clamorous peacocks congregated at the edge of the clearing. Then, she charged up the slope—only to miss her kill because, once actually among her clattering, terrified prey, she could not decide which animal to attack until all had sprung out of reach. Mouth open, panting with exertion, she stalked slowly up and over the ridge, taunted by the calls of the indignant deer.

At Ranthambhore, Fateh Singh says, it takes even the finest hunters an average of ten attempts to make a successful kill; in thicker jungles, success is said to require closer to twenty. The unusual openness of the terrain is largely responsible for this, he believes, and helps account as well for the fact that no man-eater has ever been recorded at Ranthambhore. Tigers are able to spot and stalk their normal prey with relative ease, and that prey is still plentiful; the instances of mistaken identity that often lead to the killing of humans in heavier cover elsewhere do not seem to occur here.

For more than two decades, Fateh Singh was stationed at Ranthambhore. More than any other man, he is responsible for what it has become. He is a Rajput, the proud descendant of Hindu warriors, and he brings something of his ancestors' courage and panache to his role as the tiger's champion. He struts rather than walks, and favors dark glasses and snappy, broadbrim hats. At 51, his upturned mustache has gone white, but he still sits ramrod straight in the back of the jeep, humming from sheer pleasure whenever he enters the forest he still considers his own. As we drive through the jungle, his eyes search both sides of the road for minute signs of the tiger's presence the uninitiated would never see: A few displaced pebbles tell him that a tiger has dragged its prey across the track; a single, agitated tree pie, flying in and out of dense grass, signals where the kill has been concealed.

For Fateh, even after 20 years, everything in the park still seems "fantastic"— the animals, the feathery *dhok* trees, even the ubiquitous vultures. Only the big crocodiles strain his affection. They take hours to kill the young sambar they sometimes seize, breaking first one leg, then another, biting off the tail, the ears, while the pinioned animal shrieks with fear and pain.

"Sometimes you want to shoot to end their misery," he says. "But you must not. Nature takes care of everything. Nothing must interfere with it."

That simple policy has been the secret of Fateh's success at Ranthambhore. He ended baiting and night driving within the park—though it won him few friends among visiting politicians who were no longer guaranteed to see a tiger. Most important, the villagers whose ancestors had lived in the forest for centuries were gently but firmly moved elsewhere. They did not wish to go at first; it took long nights of patient discussion with the headmen around a campfire to win their grudging acquiescence, and Fateh recalls one tearful old woman pleading to stay behind so that after she died she might be reborn as a peacock beneath the trees that shaded the only world she had ever known. But Kailashpuri, the new village he had constructed outside the park, complete with a school, temples, wells, and free, fertile land for every householder, now seems to delight his exiles. When Fateh took me to see it, schoolboys rushed to touch his feet, and young men with drums rattled out a greeting while we sipped tall glasses of sweet, milky tea.

Slowly over the years, Fateh ordered built a serpentine network of some 125 miles of roads through the forest—"the veins of my park," he calls them—enabling him to keep track of what was happening in its most remote sections. Ranthambhore Fort still shelters a temple dedicated to the elephant-headed god, Ganesh, whose blessing is sought by the pious for every sort of new undertaking, and so, on special days, as many as 10,000 barefoot pilgrims climb the metaled road that leads to the top of the hill: No tiger has ever so much as threatened any of them. Nor have tigers menaced the only permanent human residents left within the forest itself, a handful of Hindu holy men who live out of sight at the bottom of the deepest ravines and betray their presence only by the sudden, eerie blare of the conch shells they use in worship.

Otherwise, Ranthambhore belongs to the birds and animals. Tilled fields have gradually turned back into tangled forest. Deer pick their way among the deserted huts. A tigress and her cubs enjoy the shade of an old shooting tower. The deep, complacent hooting of a troop of gray langur monkeys echoes from the topmost branches of a huge pipal tree, at whose roots rests an abandoned stone deity.

Like most tigers elsewhere, those at Ranthambhore were once creatures of the night, secretive and shy. But having largely been left alone for nearly two decades, they have begun to alter their own behavior— and with it our whole notion of how these predators originally behaved. "Tigers are naturally diurnal," Valmik Thapar believes. "They became nocturnal only out of fear of man. Remove that fear, and they revert to their natural behavior." Certainly, Ranthambhore's tigers move about freely in the daytime, and by observing them for months at a time, Fateh and Valmik have managed to produce two richly illustrated, groundbreaking books on tiger behavior, and they have a third in the works.

But now this wondrous place, so painstakingly restored, is in grave danger. And its longtime defender is no longer in charge.

Ranthambhore has always been a fragile place, under constant siege. Some threats

Packed with tourists, a jeep traverses Ranthambhore's roads, as do occasional herds of encroaching livestock. Villagers drive goats toward the main gate after grazing them illegally inside the park. Local people maintain the roads; one road worker (below) shies from the camera, but not from a heavy load.

NEXT PAGES: Roads may bustle with alien creatures, but forest and savanna are the tiger's domain. A tigress streaks into the brush to chase birds from her kill.
Günter Ziesler

to its survival are traditional. Nomadic hunters camp on the fringes just long enough to send packs of lean dogs coursing after small mammals for their skins. Untouchables poach an occasional chital in hopes of making a meager profit selling the meat in the market at Sawai Madhopur. Muslim townspeople slip inside to shoot, too, because they like to serve deer on festive occasions.

The park's growing fame as the most likely place in India to see a tiger has brought with it another threat whose long-term impact is not yet fully understood. The tigers and other animals remain largely oblivious to solitary vehicles, but the number of these clamorous intruders is increasing fast: Long lines of jeeps and Land-Rovers whine through the forest, morning and evening, scattering the herds as their eager passengers lean out to shout at one another, "Have you seen the tiger? Have you seen the tiger?" Indian wildlife officials welcome tourism, foreign and domestic—for one thing, it broadens public support for conservation—but they realize the impact of uncontrolled visitation and are struggling with plans to train enough staff to deal with the growing onslaught and to teach those allowed into the forests how to behave.

Fateh drew up stringent rules for visitors to his park, but the staff has always been too small to insure that they are followed. Once a tiger is spotted, for example, no more than three jeeps are ever supposed to congregate at the site, but in practice, word of a tiger spreads instantly, and within minutes a dozen vehicles are roaring toward the spot, shrouding the roads in dust and filling the forest with the acrid smell of diesel fuel.

Even tourism can be controlled in time. The park's fate really rests in the hands of the 100,000 villagers who live on its periphery with some 200,000 head of livestock.

Like virtually all of India's parks and sanctuaries, Ranthambhore has become an island in a sea of people. Under the relent-

Before returning to a partially devoured kill, a tigress quenches her thirst. Tigers generally attack on land, but at Ranthambhore some have learned to kill in the water. Here a male leaps into a lake to pursue a sambar. If the tiger is lucky, the panicked sambar, its movements hindered by the water, will be unable to escape.

Günter Ziesler (also right)

Satiated, a male tiger rests beside his kill. Tigers camp near the remains of slain prey until, alternating between sleeping and eating, they have devoured everything edible. Scavenging vultures camp near tiger kills too but dine in a less leisurely fashion, swooping in should the tiger leave for even a moment. Screeching, tugging, and flapping, the birds feed until the tiger chases them off.

less pressure of population, the adjacent forests and grasslands where young tigers were meant to disperse have virtually disappeared, hacked down for firewood and chewed up by big haggard herds of goats, cows, and buffalo that wander through daily in search of what little greenery might have escaped them the day before.

To the villagers, the thickets and meadows of Ranthambhore represent the most convenient source of fuel and fodder, and the result has been a more or less constant state of border war between the graziers and a small force of forest guards with orders to keep them out.

A few years ago, some 50 villagers armed with clubs cornered Fateh on the border of

the park. "They decided to give me a good beating," he remembers. In fact, they left him for dead: kneecap shattered, nose broken, skull fractured. He spent three months in the hospital and was awarded India's highest civilian award for heroism. His friends advised him to leave Ranthambhore; his own mother told him he would be killed if he went back. But he did go back—to the very village from which his attackers came, driving into its center while still in plaster casts, and challenging its residents to try again. "I wanted them to see I was still alive," he remembers, "that they had done the wrong thing, but I was still willing to work together with them."

Fateh remained determined to defend his

227

Günter Ziesler (opposite)

A shared need for food and protection brings two species together. Langurs lunching in treetops are warned of a nearby tiger by the shrill cries of chital grazing below. Chital benefit even more: They gain the higher vantage point and barked warning of the langurs, and also eat any food the monkeys drop on the ground. Other langurs frequent Ranthambhore's hilltop fortress.

ramparts, but he also learned that in the long run, mere militancy would never work. The villages grew every year; so did their dependence upon the forest. Unless their needs could be changed or met some other way, unless the villagers could be made to see that the park's survival was of some direct benefit to them, it was doomed.

He and Valmik drew up an ambitious five-year plan: Local banks agreed to provide low-interest loans with which to purchase improved livestock for those villagers willing to stay out of the forest, for example, and the forest department itself would feed those new cattle on grass grown exclusively for that purpose on forest lands outside the park. Mobile educational units were to move from village to village, explaining the principles of conservation, warning of what would happen to human as well as animal life if the forests were finished off.

"We proposed that such measures be put on a war footing," Valmik remembers. "But

it was one thing to draw up a plan. Implementation was something else. Nothing was done, government priorities clashed, and things got worse. Tigers don't vote, people do, so local politicians supported grazing. Then the rains stopped."

Left alone, nature restored Ranthambhore. Now, in uneasy collaboration with man, nature threatens to destroy it. Consecutive years of drought, the worst in this century, have seared Rajasthan, shrinking Ranthambhore's famous lakes to shallow pools ringed by dried mud and withering what little fodder the already parched countryside might have offered to the villagers.

The rains will come again, of course. They always do eventually. The lakes will fill up again, and the forest will recover fully if left alone. But the ever growing numbers of people who live outside the park can't wait for nature to take its leisurely course. Ranthambhore's grass and timber now seem their last defense against disaster, and they pour across the park's borders in greater numbers than ever before.

After three years of bitter strife with villagers and local officials, during which Prime Minister Rajiv Gandhi was forced to intervene personally on the park's behalf, Fateh had become the focus of so much controversy that he was finally ordered to take up new duties elsewhere.

He refused to go. "How can I leave this place after 20 years?" he asks. "It has been my life. Whatever happens, I am here. I will never go away." He has built a farmhouse on the western edge of the park and plans to live there for the rest of his life, driving into the park every day to do what he can to keep Ranthambhore alive.

Meanwhile the daily struggle is left to his 40-year-old successor, Jaswant Singh Nathawat. "We do the best we can," he says. "But it is very difficult. The graziers used to come in small groups, no more than fifteen men at a time. One or two forest guards could take care of them. Now they

come in hundreds, sometimes thousands."

On a single day last summer, a thousand herdsmen led 15,000 hungry cattle into Ranthambhore's ravines. It took an army of policemen, home guards, and agents of the revenue department, and a pitched battle during which shots were fired, to help the forest department drive them out again.

Many of the graziers and woodcutters were back the next day, and the next. They are still coming.

One morning I asked Fateh to take me on a long drive, first along the park's borders, so that I could see for myself how the forest fares without protection, then inside, following roads most visitors never see.

We sped past mile after mile of stony hillside broken only by dusty stumps and long since emptied of all but the most tenacious wildlife. Fateh stopped to point out the spot where last year he found three dead tiger cubs, their bodies emaciated, their skulls crushed by their mother, evidently unable

to find enough natural prey to feed herself, let alone her growing offspring. He buried the cubs beneath a great banyan tree in the heart of Ranthambhore.

Despite the memory, Fateh's fierce, natural optimism seemed intact. As we started off again, he spoke of the "beautiful" rootstock still stubbornly alive beneath the seared slopes. "All this needs is a little protection, and it can be a fantastic forest again," he told me, and scattered patches of green hillside, which he had managed to shelter imperfectly with barbed wire for just a few seasons, seemed to prove him right: Even the most degraded forest can come back if given enough unmolested time.

But there is no time. We entered the park through an entrance rarely used by visitors. Fateh hadn't been in this area for weeks and was braced to see some damage, but he was clearly not ready for the devastation that was suddenly everywhere around us.

"It's a massacre," he said. Whole trees lay

Inside the ancient battlements of Ranthambhore Fort, pilgrims pass this chhatri, or pavilion (left), as they walk to and from the Ganesh Temple.

In a cave in Kamaldhar Gorge lives a holy man called the Kamaldhar Baba (opposite). He believes himself divinely shielded from the tigers and bears that share his gorge.

across the track, leaves still bright green, felled just that morning by graziers. A little farther along, six men hurried off the road and into a gully at our noisy approach, balancing great bundles of freshly cut grass on their heads as they ran. Great expanses of tall, sun-bleached grass, remembered from earlier visits, had been cropped to stubble. The half-dried droppings of cattle were scattered everywhere, big as dinner plates.

"Twenty years of work . . . gone, like that," Fateh raised one hand from the wheel in a rare, helpless gesture. "Two, three more years of this, and it will all be finished." He lapsed into uncharacteristic silence, punctuated now and again by a soft "oof," as we passed yet another despoiled thicket, another chewed-over clearing.

Toward midday we followed a twisting, rutted road that led up a long slope to the highest point in the park. We stopped on the summit near a cairn of stones on which Fateh likes to stand and survey the forest to which he has devoted his adult life.

"I haven't been to the cinema hall in 25 years," he said. "This is my cinema."

From here, Ranthambhore seemed at first as it has always been, the violet hills stretching away in all directions, the rutting calls of chital stags echoing across the slopes beneath a vast sky of unbroken blue. But as I peered more closely, I could see that some of the dark shapes browsing in the grassy clearings below were domestic buffalo, not deer; the tops of the outermost hills were strangely saw-toothed, the undergrowth already eaten away, leaving only the tallest trees standing; and broad patches of the hillsides themselves had been stripped bare.

The Ranthambhore forest is visibly retreating, its buffer zone already largely a thing of the past. Another scorching summer is soon to come. The herds will grow more voracious, their owners more desperate. And there is still no certainty of rain.

Back at Fateh's farm on the park's edge that evening, the desert air is still cold and we huddle around a fire. Despite a strong drink and the brilliant display of stars, our host is unusually quiet, still dispirited by the damage we'd seen in our daylong drive.

"We have learned that we can no longer look to government alone to solve our problems," Valmik Thapar says. "We must solve them ourselves. The local people must be made to see that the park's survival will benefit them as well as the animals. Otherwise, Ranthambhore is doomed, and so are all the other forests in India. And if the forests die, so will we all."

Valmik is working to create a private foundation to put into practice some of the schemes the overburdened government has been unable to implement: pilot projects to provide villagers with alternate sources of fuel and fodder, to involve more local people in maintaining the park. Another friend of Fateh's is encouraging villagers to revive forgotten handicrafts—brightly colored lacquer bangles, tie-dyed saris, embroidered slippers—anything that will yield enough profit to stop them from raiding the forest.

"All small projects," Valmik admits. "But we hope we can set an example for other parks throughout India."

All this will take precious time. Meanwhile, I ask, why does Fateh continue to stay on here? How can he stand by and see the forest, for which he very nearly sacrificed his life, eaten away, day after day, and be unable to do anything to stop it?

He continues to stare into the flames. "I am an Indian," he says finally. "If I die, I die, but we must not let this place die. Ranthambhore is like the Taj Mahal. It belongs to us and to our children and grandchildren. I can never leave it."

As he speaks, I grow gradually aware of what seems at first to be the rasping sound of sawing wood, coming from somewhere in the plundered forest behind me.

Fateh brightens, holds up his hand: "That's a leopard."

He jumps up from his chair, strides out beyond the circle of firelight, and, legs spread wide and head thrown back, snarls into the darkness.

The leopard answers him, and as we listen, Fateh Singh Rathore and the great, unseen cat continue to call to one another through the Rajasthan night.

By Geoffrey C. Ward
Photographs by George F. Mobley

A flock of green pigeons basks in the sun, and peacocks stand off in a ritual rarely witnessed or photographed—a battle for the attentions of a nearby peahen. The beautiful but clumsy peafowl is an easy mark for the swift tigers of Ranthambhore, and often constitutes the first successful kill in a young tiger's life.

Oceania

The myriad islands of Oceania make a kind of galaxy on earth. They swarm the Equator for most of its path across the Pacific, dividing the terrestrial sphere as spectacularly as the Milky Way divides the celestial. They array themselves in constellations: the Carolines, the Solomons, the Marquesas, the Tuamotus, the Marianas. Some are stars of the fifth magnitude, scarcely visible to the naked eye—a nameless, treeless spit of sand; crab tracks; a seabird roosting. Some are stars of the fourth magnitude—a line of palms above the beach, several roofs of thatch or tin, and a name as small as the place: Eo, Aga, Ant, Eau, Etal, Elato, Moch, Mogmog, Merir. A few are first-magnitude stars: Borneo, New Guinea, Sumatra, New Zealand. One, Australia, is sun to this system, an island so huge it makes a continent.

Oceania holds a disproportionate share of the planet's biological diversity—2,000 ecosystems in more than 20 biogeographical provinces. Ecosystems throughout Oceania are fragile. Their flora and fauna, evolved in isolation, are wonderfully idiosyncratic, whimsical, vulnerable. New Zealand's little spotted kiwi, which lost its ability to fly because it originally had no natural predators, is virtually extinct in the wild. The terrestrial biota of Hawaii, the most isolated archipelago on the planet, was once at least 96 percent endemic. Fewer than 4 percent of its species occurred elsewhere. The decline of that uniqueness

United States

Hawaii Volcanoes National Park

A curtain of fire and red-hot cinders sears earth and sky as a side vent of Kilauea erupts. Petrified rivers of black lava streak the volcano's gently sloping sides, twisting through a primeval landscape of steaming craters, stumpy vegetation, and skeletal trees. Visitors can go right up to the top of this

The early inhabitants of Oceania understood the characteristics of fragility. Islanders seem to have grasped, first of all peoples, that earthly resources are finite. The resident of Taka or Tobi, of Nama or Ngulu, could cross his island from oceanside to lagoonside in minutes. Shinnying up a coconut palm, he gained a perspective that Westerners achieved only late in this century, viewing those first NASA photographs of our blue-green planet from space.

Oceania's islanders might well argue that the first parks in the world were theirs. The residents protected their marine resources by a system of taboos, closed seasons, closed areas, size-of-catch restrictions, and gear restrictions. Limited entry was the rule. Puluwat set aside its own turtle island, Pikelot. In Pacific atolls composed of several islands, one or more was left wild and uninhabited, recruitment areas for game fish and birds. Forests, farms, and fishing grounds were owned by the family or clan. They belonged to someone, not everyone, and the owners had a vested interest in maintaining them.

With the arrival of the Europeans, the conservation ethic of Oceania met its opposite. Eager to extract timber from clan-owned forests, the colonial powers monkeyed with traditional land tenure. Eager to extract pearls and trepangs from the reefs, they vitiated traditional fishing rights. The reef now belonged to everyone, and the scramble was on to exploit it.

French Polynesia has no national parks today, nor has Fiji or Kiribati. (They have some protected areas.) The Cook Islands have dedicated one national park, Suwarrow, but it comprises just a hundred acres. There is a single national park in the Solomons, Queen Elizabeth. Hawaii has two big national parks, Haleakala and Hawaii Volcanoes. Papua New Guinea, of all Oceania's developing nations, has an impressive record in preservation, having established seven national parks and reserves, and eleven wildlife management areas. There need to be many more.

Australia

Cradle Mountain-Lake St. Clair National Park

Like characters from a science fiction thriller, tussocks of pandanus march up a hill near Lake St. Clair. Members of the heath family, these giant screw pines can grow 40 feet tall. A cross section of native plants, from majestic beeches and pines to diminutive flowers and herbs, make their home here in Tasmania's central highlands.

The 52-mile-long Overland Track—an easy walk of five or six days—links the park's namesake features. The trail skirts Lake St. Clair, Australia's deepest, then passes waterfalls in the temperate rain forest, traverses alpine moors, skirts some of Tasmania's highest peaks, and climbs past rock-walled glacial lakes en route to 5,069-foot Cradle Mountain.

Uluru (Ayers Rock-Mount Olga) National Park

Bathed in moonglow, the Olgas sprawl in the central Australian desert like beached leviathans, their smooth hide scratched by the clawings of rain and wind. Their 36 domes, made of conglomerate rock, cover 13.5 square miles. The Olgas and nearby Ayers Rock are all that remain of an ancient mountain range uplifted 600 million years ago by forces deep within the earth, then reduced to sand by wind and water, heat and cold.

Ayers Rock (opposite), 20 miles to the east, juts 1,143 feet above the sandy plain. A water hole at its base provides food and water for Aborigines who revere the red sandstone

Uluru. Their ancestors decorated about a dozen caves at its base with polychromatic wall paintings of sacred objects, legends, and rituals. Today, Aborigines own Ayers Rock protect both Ayers and the Olgas, rising in isolation in the heart of the outback.

Michael Jensen, Auscape International

Kakadu National Park

Older than the cave paintings at Lascaux in France, Kakadu's rock art chronicles 25,000 years of Aboriginal life and lore, history and ritual. Traditional X-ray art (below) reveals the subjects' skeletons; dots denote milk-filled breasts. The oldest paintings depict vanished species like the Tasmanian tiger. More recent works portray European settlers, rifles, fishing boats, and a plane.

Preserved in a 300-mile-long sandstone escarpment, this remarkable record is sacred to the Aborigines. To protect their land and their interests, they serve as park rangers. About 300 Aborigines still live in the park, hunting and fishing much as their ancestors did.

These ancestors—migrants from Southeast Asia—settled here in northern Australia well over 40,000 years ago. Some of their descendants spoke a language called Gagudju, from which the park takes its name.

For millennia, humans have exploited Kakadu's resources, some of the richest in Australia. A third of the continent's bird and plant species and a quarter of its freshwater fish species inhabit the region. Saltwater crocodiles breed in tropical tidal flats. The mangrove swamps and billabongs of the floodplain support a profusion of ducks, geese, and wading birds. Beyond rolling woodlands of palm and eucalyptus loom the sheer walls of the sandstone escarpment.

Nambung National Park

Thousands of limestone pillars rise like tombstones from the sand dunes of Nambung National Park. Called the Pinnacles, some are as high as ten feet, others as small as a pencil. Over tens of thousands of years, calcium carbonate leached from the sand and calcified around plant roots, then wind and rain sculptured the limestone into pinnacles.

The sand dunes run parallel to Australia's west coast, with the youngest and steepest dunes closest to the sea. Farther inland, kestrels hover above rolling heaths and woodlands of orange-flowered banksia trees and stunted gum trees. Gray kangaroos seek cover among thickets of stubby eucalyptus. After the rains fall from May to September, wildflowers color much of the park.

Robin Smith

241

Noriyuki Yoshida, Orion Press

New Zealand

Mount Cook National Park

Lupines spike a meadow beneath the serrated spine of the Southern Alps, which run the length of New Zealand's rugged South Island. In Mount Cook National Park alone, about 20 peaks are more than 10,000 feet high. Mount Cook itself, at 12,349 feet the country's highest, is named for the intrepid British navigator who charted New Zealand's coast in 1769. The Maori call the three-cornered, ice-sheathed monolith the "cloud in the sky." Sixty climbers have died trying to conquer it.

These are young peaks, uplifted within the last five million years. The mountains continue to rise almost half an inch a year. But glaciers erode some peaks just as quickly as they rise, so their height remains constant. Permanent snow and ice cover more than a third of the park's 270 square miles.

The park provides refuge for wildlife found only in this island nation, including the paradise shelduck, a cheeky alpine parrot called the kea, and the Mount Cook "lily"—with blooms three inches across, the largest buttercup in the world.

The Shotover River, site of a late 19th-century gold rush, flows through rugged country near Queenstown on New Zealand's South Island. A regional recreation center, Queenstown is a jumping-off point for those venturing westward into the mountains of Fiordland National Park.

Sloshing Through Paradise

Even today the water world of Fiordland National Park is almost paradise, one of the world's last wildernesses. But a thousand years ago, before the arrival of humans, it was like the world before the Fall.

Then, there were no predators except falcons, hawks, and eagles—no other meat eaters. There were no browsing mammals, no land mammals at all, apart from two species of small bat. Everything grew and flourished, and the weather came up from the Roaring Forties, watering this southwest corner of New Zealand with up to 300 inches a year. It is still one of the wettest places in the world. It was once so safe that the birds lost their sense of danger, and without enemies some stopped flying, among them the flightless New Zealand goose and the Fiordland crested penguin. Others evolved into enormous and complacent specimens, like spoiled and overfed children—the giant rail, more than a yard tall, or the feathered, long-necked moa, a distant relative of the emu and the ostrich, which grew as tall as ten feet. In that old paradise the trees grew abundantly and the moss was two feet deep—a perfect seedbed for new trees. The creatures lived on roots and insects, and not on each other. The foliage grew without being cut or grazed. Fiordland, which had been created by glaciers, was the peaceable kingdom.

When the Maori arrived, probably in the 10th century, from tropical Polynesia, with the dog (*kuri*) and the rat (*kiore*) they kept for food, they made forays into Fiordland from the north. They had a great love for decorative feathers, and in their quest for them and food they hunted many birds into extinction. The Maori dogs and rats preyed on the ground-dwelling birds. For the first time since its emergence from the Ice Age, Fiordland's natural balance was disturbed. The arrival of these predators produced the ecological equivalent of Original Sin.

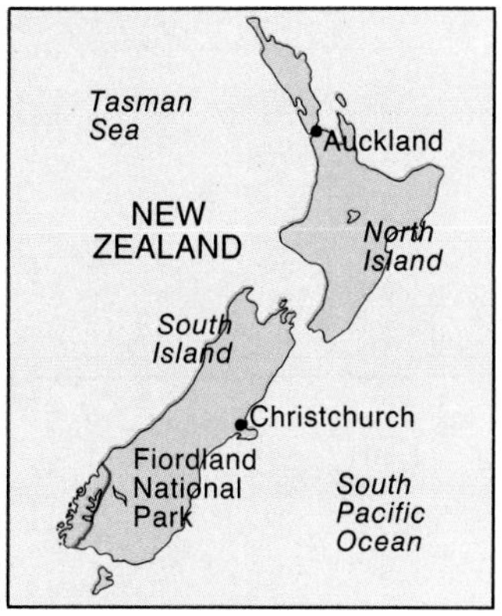

Fiordland National Park

4,678 Square Miles

Deep fiords beneath steep mountainsides indent Fiordland's wild, rain-soaked coast. Ice Age glaciers carved both the fiords and the deep lakes on the park's eastern boundary. Only one public road goes into the park; otherwise visitors enter on floatplane, boat, or shoe leather. Boats on Lake Te Anau take walkers to the newly opened Kepler Track and the famed Milford Track, claimed—not by all—to be "the finest walk in the world." The author chose the less renowned Routeburn Track, for its windswept heights and for the diversity of its views.

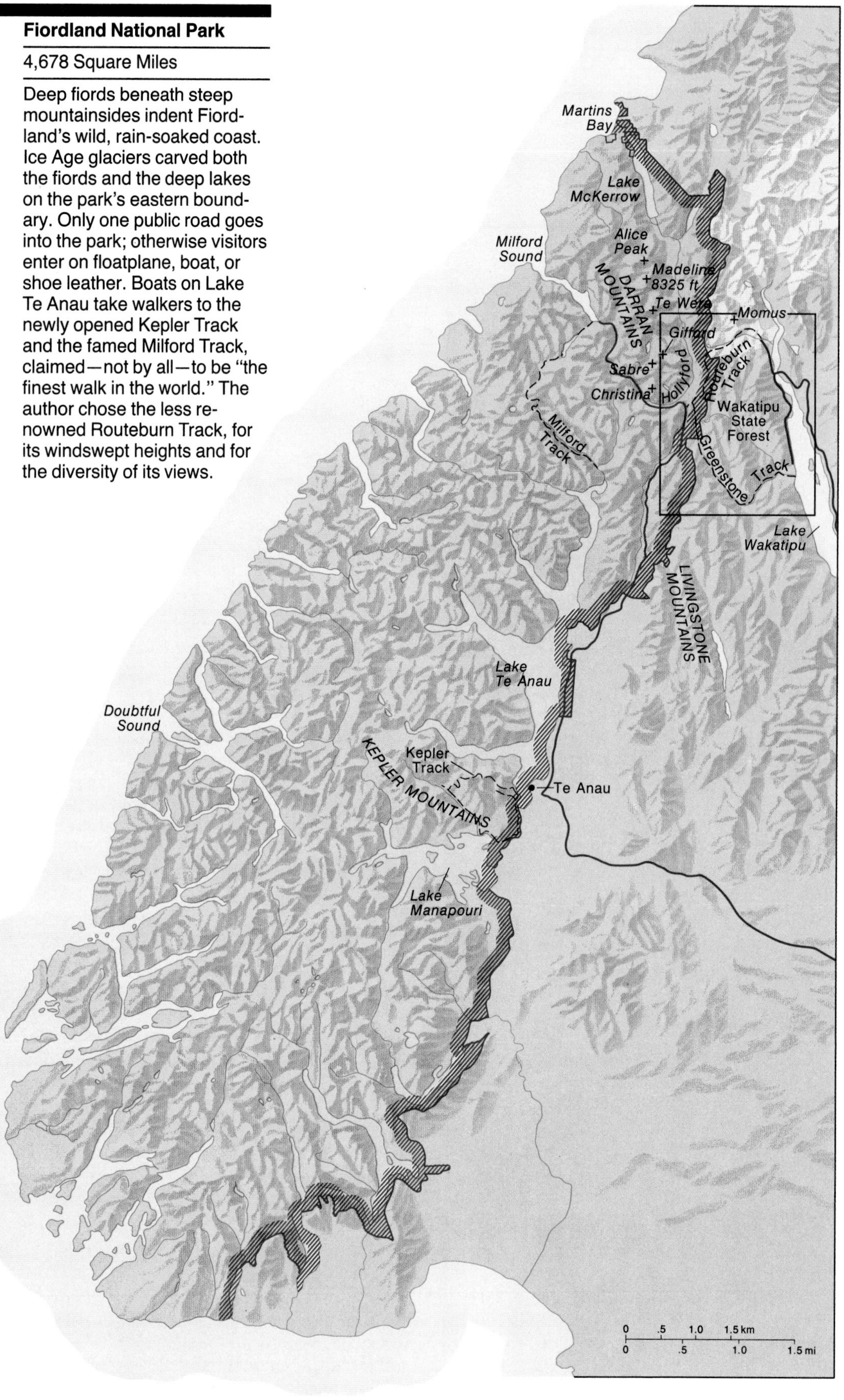

NEW ZEALAND

Tasman Sea

Auckland

North Island

South Island

Christchurch

Fiordland National Park

South Pacific Ocean

Martins Bay

Lake McKerrow

Milford Sound

Alice Peak

Madeline + 8325 ft

Te Wera

Momus +

Gifford

Sabre +

Christina +

Hollyford

Routeburn Track

Wakatipu State Forest

Milford Track

DARRAN MOUNTAINS

Greenstone Track

Lake Wakatipu

Doubtful Sound

LIVINGSTONE MOUNTAINS

Lake Te Anau

Kepler Track

KEPLER MOUNTAINS

Te Anau

Lake Manapouri

0 .5 1.0 1.5 km

0 .5 1.0 1.5 mi

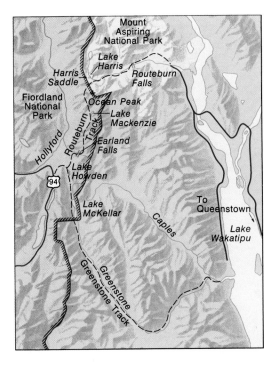

There were always treasure seekers in Fiordland—Maori looking for feathers and greenstone, colonials looking for gold—but such people were transients. Fiordland never had any permanent settlement, only camps and way stations and the temporary colonies of sealers and whalers. People came and went. Fiordland remains uninhabited, a true primeval forest.

The difficulty is that, though humans passed through, they left many of their animals behind. They introduced various species either for sport or food, or in the mistaken belief that one animal would stabilize another. This brought a subtle chaos to Fiordland. The stoats and weasels were supposed to keep the rabbits in check, but instead they ate birds and their eggs and the rabbits increased. The same story was repeated for every other nonnative creature.

"The major threat to vegetation is the red deer," the district conservator of Fiordland, Terry Pellett, told me. "The deer are every-where." In the past, he said, helicopters flying over almost inaccessible hanging valleys could see 300 or 400 deer in the steepest places. "The Norway rats that came to New Zealand on ships have multiplied and reduced the native bird population. We have American elk, the only herd in the Southern Hemisphere. They're also a nuisance. There are so many exotic species that thrive here and harm the local flora and fauna—possums, chamois, and hares."

The great debate continues in Fiordland over what is native and what is alien. For ecological reasons, the protectors and well-wishers of this area are wary of all strangers—plant and animal. It is park policy to eliminate or reduce these exotic species of animals. It is always open season on deer. And a note of disgust enters the voice of normally placid New Zealanders who want to see an end to the vast tracts of the immigrant species of trees. Foreign trees are regarded as unsightly weeds, whether they are Douglas fir, silver birch, or spruce, and no growing things are hated more than the rampant gorse and broom planted by sentimental and homesick Scots.

Nearly all the people I met said they wanted to reclaim their hills and make them bald and bright again, ridding them of these alien plants and animals, to bring about the resurgence of the flightless birds, vegetarians, and insectivores, and to preserve the long valleys of native conifers and beeches. There have been some pleasant surprises. One guileless, ground-dwelling bird, the plump, beaky takahe, which the Maori hunted, was thought to be extinct. In 1948 some takahes were found in a remote region of Fiordland. Although protected, the bird still faces an uncertain future.

Old habits of contentment, curiosity, and trust—the legacy of paradise—remain among many bird species in Fiordland. Anyone taking a walk through the rain forests will be followed by the South Island robin, the fantail, the tomtit, and the tiny

rifleman, New Zealand's smallest bird. These birds seem absolutely without fear and will flutter and light a few feet away, pecking at insects the hiker has disturbed. The kea, or mountain parrot, is so confident it becomes an intruder, squawking its own name and poking into your knapsack.

So, in magnificent Fiordland, where the birds are unafraid and all the water is drinkable, the birdwatcher doesn't need binoculars and the hiker has no use for a canteen.

The most famous long-distance walk in Fiordland is the Milford Track, but it is now a victim of marketing success, and "the finest walk in the world" is simply hyperbole. It has become crowded and intensively regulated, and as a result rather hackneyed.

But the Routeburn was my choice for autumn in Fiordland, because—unlike the Milford, which is essentially a valley walk with one high climb—it rises to well above the scrub line and stays there, circling the heights, offering vistas of the whole northeast corner of Fiordland. And the Routeburn can be combined with the Greenstone Valley Walk, allowing a full week's walking—entering and leaving Fiordland the way people have done for centuries, on foot.

There is an intense but simple thrill in setting off in the morning on a mountain trail knowing that everything you need is on your back. It is a confidence in having left all inessentials behind, and of entering a world of natural beauty which has not been violated, where money has no value and possessions are a deadweight. The person with the fewest possessions is the freest: Thoreau was right. It seems fanciful to say that I felt a lightness of spirit, but the feeling was real, and physically real as well, and so powerful it had the effect of easing my load. From the age of nine or ten, when I first began hiking, I have associated camping with personal freedom. My pleasure has intensified over the years as equipment has improved and become more manageable and efficient. When I was very young,

camping equipment was just another name for "war surplus." Everything was canvas. Now the stuff is colorful and almost stylish.

And hikers are no longer middle-aged Boy Scouts. A violinist, a factory worker, an aspiring actor, a photographer, a food writer, a broadcaster, a student, and a grumpy little man with an East European accent made up our Routeburn hiking party. We were, I suppose, representative. Some dropped by the wayside; the photographer stayed on at one hut to take pictures, and the man who kept interrupting discussion with, "Hah! You sink so! You must be choking!" at last went home, and when we finished the Routeburn, only three of us pushed on to the Greenstone. The violinist stayed the whole week, quietly cursing the water and mud. The broadcaster was solicitous toward me—and I toward her: Well, we are married. The violinist apologized for being a slow walker, but he was better at other pursuits—he was concertmaster of the New Zealand Symphony Orchestra, and he had a knack for beating me at Scrabble during the long nights at the trackside shelters.

The Routeburn Track starts at the north end of Lake Wakatipu in an area full of deer and majestic stags. I find it hard to view these creatures, as the New Zealanders do, as pests. Vermin is not the first thing that comes to mind when you see the monarch of the glen. I set off through the beech forest and tramped along a shady rising path. The other hikers were widely scattered, but we met for lunch beside a stream (which we drank from). We were bitten by sand flies, one of Fiordland's few nuisances, easily discouraged with a squirt of insect repellent. After a horizontal stretch across Routeburn Flats, among the tawny blowing tussocks, we climbed steeply on a track that took us through gnarled and ancient beeches to Routeburn Falls. This is a succession of cataracts which cascade over black rocks on about six levels of bouldery terraces.

From this altitude, looking west, it is possible to see clearly how the glaciers carved Fiordland, creating the characteristic U-shaped valleys, whose sheer walls give them the illusion of even greater height. The dragging and abrasive glaciers smoothed the valleys' walls, but here the ice was about 5,000 feet thick, and so the tops of the mountains are jagged and sharp where the glacier didn't reach.

A hut on the Routeburn Track is essentially a small, drafty shelter erected over a Scrabble board. At the Routeburn Falls hut that first night we discovered each other's profession and personality, and as we talked the rain began to patter on the roof.

"How did the Maori withstand this cold?" someone asked.

James Hayward, the aspiring actor, did not always have the most accurate explanations, but they were the most memorable.

"The Maori kept warm by catching keas," he said, referring to the mountain parrots. "They hollowed out these birds and strapped them to their feet and used them for slippers."

"I sink you are choking," came a voice. "Hah!"

James merely smiled.

Someone else said, "Hadn't Maori sandals been found on the trail?"

"You see a lot of interesting things on the trail," James said. "I once saw a man on the Routeburn in a bowler hat, a pin-striped suit, a tightly rolled umbrella, and all his gear in a briefcase."

He had had to raise his voice, for the wind and rain had increased. It kept up all night, falling fast and turning to sleet and making a great commotion, with constant smashing sounds, pushing the side of the hut and slapping the window. It was still driving down hard in the morning. Visibility was poor. Between swirling cloud and glissades of sleet, I could see that it had left deep new snow on the summit of Momus and other nearby mountains. From every mountainside cataracts erupted, milky white, spurt-ing down the steep black rock faces.

"Let's go walkabout," James said.

We left the hut and tramped up the path in the snowy rain and wind, marveling at how the Routeburn Falls was now about twice the torrent it had been the day before. The narrow footpath coursed with water, and I had wet feet before I had gone ten yards. We climbed for an hour to a hilltop lake that lay in a rocky bowl, a body of water known here, and in Scotland, as a tarn. ("Burn" is also Scottish for that matter, meaning "stream.") The storm crashed into the tarn for a while, but even as we watched, it lessened and soon ceased altogether. Within 15 minutes the sun came out and blazed powerfully—brighter than any sunlight I had ever seen. "This sunlight is three-quarters of a stop brighter than anywhere else on earth I've been," the photographer Ian Berry said.

In this dazzling light we climbed onward to Lake Harris, a greeny blue lake enclosed by cliffs. Then we were above it, tramping through alpine scrub and the blowing spear grass they call spaniard, and soon we were at Harris Saddle (4,200 feet), which stands as a glorious gateway to Fiordland. Beyond it is the deep Hollyford Valley, which winds to the sea, and high on its far side the lovely Darran Mountains, with glaciers still slipping from their heights and new snow whipping from their ridges.

The Harris Saddle is worth the long climb for its panorama of summits to the west, a succession of mile-high mountains—Christina, Sabre, Gifford, Te Wera, and Madeline. I could not imagine mountains packed more tightly than this—a whole ocean of peaks.

Apart from the wind whispering in the stunted scrub, there was silence here. At this height, among powerful mountains, one has left the mean and vulgar far behind and has entered a world without pettiness. Its counterpart, and a feeling it closely resembles, is that soaring sense of well-being inspired by a Gothic cathedral.

We had gotten a late start because of the gale, and so we could not linger. Some went back to the falls, and the rest of us pushed on. The drama of this walk is increased by the long open climb to the saddle and the extensive traverse across the high Hollyford Face—three hours without shelter, exposed to the wind but also exposed to the beauty of the ranges—the forest, the snow, and a glimpse of the sea. It was more than 3,000 feet straight down, from the path on these cliffs to the Hollyford River on the valley floor. Our track was rocky and deceptive, and it was bordered with alpine plants—daisies, snowberries, and white gentians.

Ocean Peak was above us as we moved slowly across the rock face. It was not very late, but these mountains are so high the sun drops behind them in the afternoon, and without it we were cold. The southerly wind was blowing from Antarctica. As the day darkened, we came to a bluff, and beneath us in a new valley was a green lake. We were at such an altitude that it took us another hour to descend the zigzag path.

Deeper in the valley we were among ancient trees; and that last half hour, before darkness fell, was like a walk through an enchanted forest, the trees as old as the hills, grotesquely twisted and very damp and pungent. A forest that is more than a thousand years old, and that has never been touched or interfered with, has a ghostly look of layer upon layer of living things, and the whole forest clinging together—roots and trunks and branches mingled with moss and rocks, and everything above ground hung with tufts of lichen called old man's beard. It was so dark and damp here that moss grew on all sides of the trunks— the sunlight hardly struck them. The moss softened them and made them look like huge, tired, and misshapen monsters with great spongy arms. Everything was padded and wrapped because of the dampness, and the boughs were blackish green; the forest

Two walkers on the Route-burn head for Fiordland across an alpine meadow in Mount Aspiring National Park. A Japanese visitor crosses a swing bridge—often the only way over streams that can turn to torrents with a passing rainstorm.

NEXT PAGES: Wavelets on Lake Wakatipu suggest the odd tide-like phenomenon called a seiche. Every few minutes, the waterline may fluctuate by about five inches, due to wind or variations in atmospheric pressure over parts of the lake.

floor was deep in ferns, and every protruding rock was upholstered in velvety moss. Here and there was a chuckle of water running among the roots and ferns. We were followed by friendly robins.

It was all visibly alive and wonderful, and in places had a subterranean gleam of wetness. It was like a forest in a fairy story, the pretty and perfect wilderness of sprites and fairies, which is the child's version of paradise—a lovely Disneyish glade where birds eat out of your hand and you know you will come to no harm.

It was cold that night—freezing in fact. We woke in Mackenzie Hut to frosty bushes and icy grass and whitened ferns. There was lacework everywhere, and the sound of

a far-off waterfall that was like the howl of city traffic.

There were keas screaming overhead as we spent that day hiking—for the fun of it—to the head of Lake Mackenzie. The paradise shelducks objected to our invading their territory, and they gave their two-toned complaint—the male duck honking, the female squawking. We continued up the valley, boulder-hopping much of the way along a dry creek bed. It was steep: Most of the boulders were four or five feet thick, so it was slowgoing. We were less than halfway when we stopped for lunch, sheltered by a rock the size of a garage. The wind rose, the clouds grew lumpier and crowded the sky, and two of our already

small party turned back to the hut. The day darkened and turned cold.

Four of us climbed higher, and an hour or so later, at the highest point of the valley face, an uplifted platform just under Fraser Col, the clouds bulged and snow began to fall. We were in a large, quarrylike place littered with boulders as big as bungalows, in a gusting wind. We did not linger there. The most common emergency in these parts is not a fall or a broken limb but rather an attack of hypothermia. We descended quickly, moving from rock to rock, to whip up our blood, and we arrived back at the hut exhausted after what was to have been our rest day.

That night was typical of a stop at a trail hut. Over dinner we discussed murder, race relations, AIDS, nuclear testing, the greenhouse effect, Third World economies, the Maori claim to New Zealand, the presidential election in the United States, and Martin Luther King Day—one oaf boasting that he made a point of ignoring the day, until an acrimonious argument started. After that, we did the dishes, played Scrabble, compared blisters, and turned into the bunk room at about ten o'clock, while outside in the heavy mist an owl hooted, "More pork!" All the birds knew their names in Fiordland.

I saw a New Zealand pigeon the next morning. It was like no other pigeon in the world, fat as a football and so clumsy you wonder how it stays aloft. It does so with a

The Greenstone Track etches its way across a talus slope in the Greenstone Valley. The stones slowly accumulate as erosion by wind and water eats away at the steep, glacier-cut walls of the valley.

loud thrashing of wings. The Maori who walked this way snared these *kereru* and ate them, sustaining themselves in their search for the godly greenstone, a nephritic jade hard enough to use for implements and lovely enough for jewelry. On that same stretch, from Mackenzie to Lake Howden, I heard a bellbird. This remarkable mimicking bird trills and then growls and grates before bursting into song. It was much admired by the Maori. At the birth of a son they cooked a bellbird in a sacred oven in a ritual of sacrifice meant to insure that the child had fluency and a fine voice.

The light rain in the morning increased to a soaking drizzle until the last mile on the Routeburn Track was a muddy creek. We passed under Earland Falls, which splashes 300 feet down—the water coursing onto the rocky path. There was water and mist and noise everywhere, and it was a sort of baptism to proceed. Farther down the track the woods offered some protection from the rain, and yet we arrived at Howden Hut drenched. That is normal for Fiordland. Photography cannot do justice to rain, and so most photographs of Fiordland depict a sunny wilderness. But that sunshine is exceptional. At Lake Howden, for example, there are roughly 200 rain days a year, producing 25 feet of rain.

It was still raining in the afternoon, and yet I was looking forward to three more days walking, down the Greenstone Valley to Lake Wakatipu. We remaining three Routeburn refugees joined another group of walkers, who were clean and dry after only an hour into the trail. But after another hour they were just as wet and muddy as we.

It was the sort of rain that makes local enthusiasts start their explanations with *if only*—"If only it weren't so misty you'd be able to see wonderful—"

Wonderful peaks, lakes, forests, cliffs, waterfalls, ridges, saddles, and ravines. They were all obscured by the rain. But the wonderful woods with their mossy grottoes

Walker's reward: a view of Lake Howden (right) from Howden Hut, where the Routeburn and Greenstone Tracks meet. Nearby, Earland Falls (below) provides a refreshing—if icy—shower. The falls freeze in the winter and dwindle to a trickle during the rare summer droughts that may last as long as six weeks.

were enough. This was a famous valley, one that had been pushed open when a glacier split off from the Hollyford Valley and flowed southeast about 30 miles to Lake Wakatipu. It was another Maori route to the greenstone deposits at the top of the lake. Its presence so near the rivers and lake confirmed them in their belief that the stone was a petrified fish. Greenstone had both spiritual and material significance and was cherished because it was difficult to obtain.

Some people in this Greenstone Valley party found the rain a discouragement—it didn't rain this much in Pasadena, they said, and turned back. The rest of us carried on in a straggling and companionable way—a lawyer, a college administrator, an iron ore digger and his young son, an office clerk, an athlete, and (panting and gasping) Isidor the violinist.

The Greenstone Huts were spacious and warm. It seemed a wetter walk than the Routeburn, but at the end of the day it was easier to dry off. Seeing the sleeping arrangements, one of the Americans exclaimed, "Oh, I get it. It's bisexual."

Not exactly—but we knew what he meant. After the comradeship of the trail, there seemed little point in needlessly segregating ourselves at night. And actually nothing looks more proper—and even prim—than a dozen hikers, men and women, tucked up separately in their sleeping bags. It was a mixed bunk room.

By now we had established a pleasant routine—waking to a big breakfast of porridge and eggs, and beans on toast; and then hiking until midmorning, with a rest stop for scroggin (nuts and raisins); and then onward through the forest for lunch—on the Greenstone it was always a picnic by the drinkable river; and finally slogging throughout most of the afternoon toward one of the huts. We walked through the woods and across meadows of dry tussocks packed with pale gray and aptly named coral lichen. As the valley widened to a mile or

two, the river became louder and frothier, and the soaked graywacke stone that lay in it made it greener. Cataracts poured from the mountains above us, but they were so high and the wind so strong that they were blown aside like vaporizing bridal veils—a gauze of mist that vanished before it reached the valley floor. We were followed by birds and watched by deer and hawks and falcons. The weather was too changeable and the prevailing westerlies too strong to assure one completely rainy—or sunny— day. Clouds were always in rapid motion above us and being torn apart by the Livingstone Mountains at the edge of Fiordland— for we had now left the park proper and were making our way through Wakatipu State Forest to the lake.

The silver beeches of the high altitudes gave way to the thicker, taller red beeches of the valley and the slender and strange young lancewood trees with their downward slanting leaves at the margin of the valley floor. We walked across the sluices of long-ago rockslides and through a forest of whitened trunks of trees killed by a recent fire, and by a deep gorge and a rock (called a roche moutonnée) too stubborn for the glacier to budge, and through cool mossy woods, and knee deep in a freezing creek, always followed by birds.

At the last swing bridge that trembled like an Inca walkway near the mouth of the Greenstone, where the Caples Valley con-

verges to form an amphitheater of mountainsides, the foliage was of a European and transplanted kind—tall poplars in autumnal gold, standing like titanic ears of corn, and dark Douglas fir and the startling red leaves of copper beeches—the trees New Zealanders call foreign weeds.

I was sorry to reach the end of the trail, because there is something purifying about an experience of wilderness. To see a land in the state in which it has existed since it rose from the waters and let slip its ice, a land untouched, unchanged, its only alteration a footpath so narrow your elbows are forever brushing against ferns and old boughs, is greatly reassuring to the spirit. Such a trip stimulates the imagination and

Rain-dark skies brood over a farmstead, or station, on the way to the Routeburn trailhead. On the porch at Mackenzie Lodge (upper), hiking clothes dry in a burst of welcome sunlight. The emergency shelter at Harris Saddle, loftiest point on the Routeburn, offers refuge when storms bring snow and 70-mile-per-hour winds.

puts human effort into perspective. The smaller one feels on the earth, dwarfed by mountains and assailed by weather, the more respectful one has to be; and unless we are very arrogant, the less likely we are to poison or destroy it. Come to think of it, it is almost invariably the urban-dwelling people—out of touch with wilderness—who feel they can test atom bombs willy-nilly in fragile atolls, or dig open-pit mines in beauty spots, or cut down rain forests and deflower the wilderness. Ignorance and inexperience allow people to think that they can change the wilderness without doing irreversible harm to the planet. Fiordland is not fragile, but it is destructible.

I hated leaving Fiordland, and even as I was leaving, I was planning a return trip—to take a kayak up Lake Te Anau and into the deep twisted fiords on the western side of the lake; to walk it in winter, with crampons and an ice ax; to complete the Kepler Track—I bush-bashed a third of it, on an Easter Sunday, seeing it as an alternative to churchgoing. Te Tapu Nui the Maori called some of their mountains—"the peaks of intense sacredness."

In the meantime I was content. I was glad the park authorities were strict and that they made no exceptions to their rules; glad the tracks were narrow and steep and contained the walkers, preventing them from ranging very far; inexpressibly glad that there would never be a hotel on the Harris Saddle or a condo on the Hollyford Face or a marina on Lake Mackenzie; very glad that the wagon road that had been planned for the Greenstone Valley in 1881 had never been built; glad that the furbearing seals which frolicked in the fiords on the west coast were now a protected and secure species, with a population in Fiordland of about 14,000; glad that this magnificent place would endure. As long as there is wilderness, there is hope.

By Paul Theroux
Photographs by Ian Berry

Flaxen clumps of tussock grass dot the floodplain of the Greenstone River. As climax vegetation—the end result of a developing meadow —the grass is a prominent feature of the South Island landscape. The tall tufts shelter a variety of smaller plants from wind and sun.

A snorkeler enters one of earth's last frontiers: the watery realm of fish and coral of Australia's Great Barrier Reef. Coral reefs harbor more species of fish than any other habitat in the sea —and more species of animals than any habitat on land, even the rain forest.

Great Barrier Reef Marine Park

Under, Down Under

Auriga Bay rode at anchor in the lee of Great Detached Reef, her bow to the southeast wind. Except for a few small clouds hurrying, the Australian sky was blue. Sky and ocean flowed away to the northwest, and the boat made the only fixed point in all creation. I could smell the faint intertidal scent of coral. The surf was breaking white on reefs across 200 degrees of horizon.

The wheelhouse was empty, except for me. I slid my legs under the cramped dining table and opened my notebook. The page was blank, ready to be filled. I paused to admire the table's still life: my notebook, open and waiting. Grant's *Guide to Fishes*, closed. Photographer David Doubilet's decompression meter, lying beside his daughter Emily's paint box, her sopping brushes, her scattered half-dry art.

The watercolorist Emily Doubilet is a naïf and a primitive. She is three and a half. This afternoon she had busied herself painting a big school of blue fish with orange eyes. Anywhere else, fish like those would have seemed whimsical, but the Great Barrier Reef is a biological province as diverse and colorful as any on earth. Almost every fish form and hue conceivable—even in the imagination of a three-year-old—has actual existence here. Chances were good that fish exactly like Emily's went about their business somewhere beneath us.

I really am on the Great Barrier Reef, I thought. It was one of those sudden, week-late revelations that can come in the jet age to a traveler on the wrong side of the world.

"Great Barrier Reef" is a powerful phrase for anyone—all three component words are evocative and strong—but for me the name has a special force. The first research paper I ever wrote, for Miss Marliave in the sixth grade, was on the Great Barrier Reef. I have little memory of what I wrote and no idea why I picked the reef, but ever after I have had a proprietary interest. The Great Barrier Reef has been mine, as any subject becomes yours when you have staked it out in a literary way—especially your first.

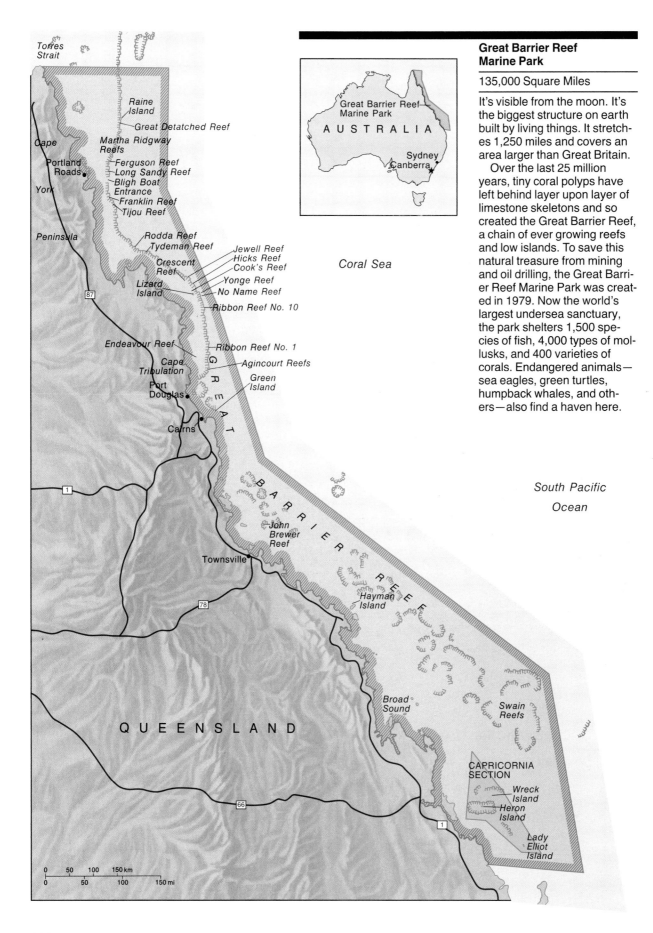

Torres
Strait

Raine
Island

Great Detatched Reef

Martha Ridgway
Reefs

Cape

Portland
Roads

Ferguson Reef

York

Long Sandy Reef

Bligh Boat
Entrance

Franklin Reef

Tijou Reef

Peninsula

Rodda Reef

Tydeman Reef

Jewell Reef

Hicks Reef

Cook's Reef

Crescent
Reef

Yonge Reef

Lizard
Island

No Name Reef

Ribbon Reef No. 10

Endeavour Reef

Ribbon Reef No. 1

Cape
Tribulation

Agincourt Reefs

Port
Douglas

Green
Island

Cairns

Coral Sea

John
Brewer
Reef

Townsville

Hayman
Island

South Pacific

Ocean

QUEENSLAND

Broad
Sound

Swain
Reefs

CAPRICORNIA
SECTION

Wreck
Island

Heron
Island

Lady
Elliot
Island

GREAT BARRIER REEF

0   50   100   150 km
0   50   100   150 mi

Great Barrier Reef
Marine Park

AUSTRALIA

Sydney
Canberra

Great Barrier Reef Marine Park

135,000 Square Miles

It's visible from the moon. It's the biggest structure on earth built by living things. It stretches 1,250 miles and covers an area larger than Great Britain.

Over the last 25 million years, tiny coral polyps have left behind layer upon layer of limestone skeletons and so created the Great Barrier Reef, a chain of ever growing reefs and low islands. To save this natural treasure from mining and oil drilling, the Great Barrier Reef Marine Park was created in 1979. Now the world's largest undersea sanctuary, the park shelters 1,500 species of fish, 4,000 types of mollusks, and 400 varieties of corals. Endangered animals— sea eagles, green turtles, humpback whales, and others—also find a haven here.

268

Ribbon Reef No. 10, longest of the outer reefs, sweeps toward the horizon. A reef is born when coral larvae attach to the ocean bottom and grow into colonies running parallel to the coast. Nourished by sun and surf, the corals on the seaward side multiply faster than those on the coastal side. There, all but hardy, slow-growing species die off, leaving behind a limestone skeleton that is gradually ground down to fine sand.

Thirty years afterward, asked to write about the reef, I accepted without hesitation. I would do a reprise of my first literary effort, that old sixth-grade paper. I would make corrections, fill in holes.

In the wheelhouse of *Auriga Bay,* I dreamed up a working title for the chapter. It would mean nothing to anyone else, but I liked it. In my notebook I jotted it down: "Report to Miss Marliave."

The Great Barrier Reef is the largest coral reef province and richest marine habitat on the planet. It is the biggest structure created by living things on earth. The reef is 1,250 miles long and is composed of 2,900 reef complexes, some very small, some as large as 40 square miles. About 400 species

of corals and 1,500 species of fish are known from the reef, and countless species of coralline algae, crustaceans, worms, mollusks, and echinoderms. Many of the reef's organisms are unknown to science, and its workings remain for the most part a mystery.

In 1975 the Australian Commonwealth government enacted its Great Barrier Reef Marine Park Act, and in 1979 the first unit of the park—the Capricornia Section, in the south—was proclaimed. The Capricorn, Central, Cairns, Far Northern, Cormorant Pass, and Mackay Sections have followed. The marine park is a somewhat bewildering patchwork of management zones: General Use 'A' (where trawling is permitted), General Use 'B' (where trawling is not), Marine

National Park 'A' and 'B' Zones, scientific research zones, preservation zones, replenishment areas, seasonal closure areas. The complexity is less than ideal, perhaps, but a kind of organic rationale underlies it. Coral reefs themselves are patchy places, their zonations complex, their regimes overlapping. At present, nearly all 2,900 reef complexes are protected by the park. The marine park, like the reef itself, has a life of its own and continues to grow.

My sixth-grade report on the reef was written under a few misimpressions, I'm afraid. For me the word "barrier" suggested a more or less continuous rampart off Australia's coast. In fact, the Great Barrier Reef is both less and more than that. In the farthest north, opposite Cape York, the reefs of the Great Barrier are deltaic reefs—less like barriers than like chains of sandy river deltas from some vanished continent. For much of its southern length, the reef is less a barrier than a maze. Fortunately I visited the Far Northern Section first. These are high-energy reefs: long, narrow, meandering, steep-walled formations along which the surf breaks creamily.

Eleven of us, crew and passengers, set out in *Auriga Bay* from Portland Roads, a depopulate little harbor on the Cape York Peninsula. The reefs of the park's Far Northern Section lie close to the Queensland coast. They are the least visited reefs, and for weeks we would see no other boat.

Our first dive was on a coral head at Mantis Reef. I had not been diving for several years, but my old, eighth-inch wet suit still fit, and it felt good—I had nearly forgotten the way a wet suit makes you feel tighter, sleeker, and more muscular than you really are. I buckled on weight belt, decompression meter, vest, and tank, and under the growing weight felt myself rapidly aging. I had nearly forgotten the awkward duckwalk in fins to the side of the boat. Then the giant stride outward. Then the splash. Then all awkwardness departing. Locomotion in

Near Raine Island, a school of many-lined sweetlips cruises over colonies of staghorn coral. These two-foot-long fish, sometimes called rubberlips, live only in the tropical waters from Japan to northern Australia.

scuba gear and fins is less like swimming than like the slow flying you do in dreams. I kicked down toward the *bommie*.

"Bommie" or "bombie" is short for *bombora*, an Aboriginal word for coral boulder. Of the Australianisms one encounters on the reef—"trevallies" for the fish Americans call jacks, "groper" for grouper, "dingo fish" for barracuda, "gnashers" for sharks generally, "white pointer" for the great white— bombora is the most indispensable, the one sure to enter a visitor's vocabulary. The word has the full, swelling, rotund shape of the thing it describes.

It was wonderful to be down under, Down Under. A school of parrotfish passed, a few digressing to munch on the coral rock, and I heard the gritty grinding of parrotfish beaks. The parrotfish were opaline—a pale, luminous blue-green shot with highlights of yellow and pink. Australia is famous for the opals of its mines; here were the living opals of its reefs. Now and then the parrotfish would defecate pellets of fine-ground coral rock. The pellets settled, disintegrating to leave trails like sandy comets.

A clown fish did its sensual dance atop an anemone, bathing in the tentacles, caressing and being caressed. It was continually renewing acquaintance with its host, immunizing itself against the stinging cells that protected it. The clown fish was barred behind the eye and at the chest in Day-Glo bands of a lovely pale lavender. An angelfish shied away into a crevice, its nose to the rock, its tail out. A white-tip reef shark cruised by—an unaggressive species, but good, as always, for a momentary shock. Several unicornfish passed. A Moorish idol. A black-spotted toadfish. Surgeonfish of several varieties. A lizardfish.

Two pipefish, eel-like relatives of the sea horse, flowed away over the convolutions of a brain coral. They were translucent and no thicker than darning needles. At one end was a paddle-like caudal fin, at the other a minuscule sea dragon's head. The tiny eyes rotated independently on their stalks to look back at me. No matter how hard I tried to separate the two fish with my finger, they stuck together. How, I wondered, could so much fidelity fit in so small a package?

A blue-spotted stingray rested on the sand beneath a coral overhang. Keeping clear of the barb at the base of the tail, I stared into the devilish eye. The stingray's spots seemed *projected* on its head and wings, as if from some very bright, intensely blue external source. The spots were the same illusory electric blue as those you see when standing up too suddenly.

I felt the disequilibrium that comes on me on coral reefs. The reef is a system too complex, too diverse. An eye and brain trained in the temperate zone is overwhelmed by it. There are too many shapes and colors, too many things to see, too many questions.

On *Auriga Bay* we quickly learned the past histories of our shipmates, as one does on a small boat. Graham McCallum, the captain, was from South Australia, where he had been a fisherman, abalone diver, ketch skipper, and insurance salesman. None of that had been quite right. On the Great Barrier Reef, skippering dive boats, he finally had found the life that agreed with him. He did seem right for the job: a big, tanned, garrulous, affectionate, opinionated character whose pleasure was other people's enjoyment of the reef. Until wandering to the Great Barrier, he had been like one of those coral planulae adrift in the plankton, its life on hold, waiting for the right substrate on which to settle.

"When you dive the same spots, you begin to know the individual fish," Elaine McCallum, Graham's wife, told me. "Think of them as your *mates*." She laughed. "That's silly, isn't it? They're just fish!"

If the McCallums were resident organisms, then Rodney Fox and his family were migrants, occasional visitors like the reef's marlins or leatherback turtles. Rodney is a former champion spear-fisherman and abalone diver from South Australia. As a young man he was attacked by a great white shark, the epochal event in his life. The shark bit but did not chew. It left Rodney with his insides rearranged, horrific scars on his torso, and a fascination with the great predator that nearly killed him. He was a man full of pleasure in small things—a pleasure that comes when a great white shark has relented and returned your life to you.

As an 11-year-old scholar, writing for the first time on the Great Barrier Reef, I was under the impression the whole thing was underwater. In fact, the ocean sometimes heaps sand islets on top of the reef. Australians call these reef islets "cays." They are few and far between, but 300 Great Barrier reefs have managed to produce them.

Our northernmost goal was a cay called Raine Island. Most sand cays are bare, guano-spattered, sunbaked places devoid of human history. Raine is different. A stone tower stands on the island, a monument to the vanity of human endeavor.

In August 1834 the British bark *Charles Eaton* wrecked on Great Detached Reef, south of Raine. That wreck, and others in the northern reef, caused the British government in 1843 to dispatch Captain Blackwood and H.M.S. *Fly* to the area. Blackwood was to find a site for a tower that would mark a safe passage through the reefs, guiding ships in from the Coral Sea. He chose Raine Island and in 1844 returned with 20 convict masons. The convicts quarried coral rock from the island, salvaged timbers from the wreck of *Martha Ridgway,* made mortar from the reef's shells, and at the end of four months had erected a tower 64 feet high.

Their labors were for very little, in the end. The Raine Island tower was never needed. Soon after its construction, a better route was discovered through the reefs, and the tower became obsolete.

When we first sighted the tower from *Auriga Bay,* 143 years later, it was a pale point on the horizon. We had trouble finding it again if we looked away. Steadily the tower grew taller. Through my binoculars I could make out a smoky cloud of birds over the tower, then I could discern the wheeling dots of individual birds; finally I recognized the birds as frigates. The tower had a fascination, both for me and for the birds. It stood like one of those "vast and trunkless legs of stone" of the Shelley poem, except that it was surrounded not by desert but by a wilderness of reefs.

All around us birds were winging home from the sea: brown boobies skimming the surface in great numbers; masked boobies sailing in a little higher; sooty terns, white-capped noddy terns, and crested terns higher still; and frigatebirds highest of all. The smell of guano was acrid and strong. "After an hour or two, you don't smell it anymore," Graham advised us. That was no particular consolation to me. I love bird islands. I *like* the smell of guano.

Photographer Dave Doubilet, anxious to get underwater, readied his cameras for the first dive. The universe above the surface interests Doubilet only marginally. I myself have some affection for land, so I snorkeled in to the beach. Sitting up in shallow water, I pulled off my fins and mask and stood— terra firma again. The island was all mine.

Nesting green turtles had bulldozed the entire foreslope of the beach, then rebull-dozed it, tracks on top of tracks. Behind the beach crest, in digging the deep bowls of their nests and throwing up hills of excavated sand, the turtles had left a choppy landscape of small dunes and hollows. Raine Island is annually assaulted by the densest aggregations of nesting green turtles on earth. Eleven thousand turtles were once counted in a single night on Raine.

Now, in late morning, a few turtles struggled back down to the water. They dragged the great weight of themselves, rested, then dragged again. They labored silently, except for an occasional weary exhalation.

Like a big blue ball, fusiliers roll along the reef bottom. Schooling for protection by day, at night the fish retire, one by one, into caves or the recesses of coral, like the soft coral below. The lionfish (left), which grows 15 inches long, defends itself by inflicting painful wounds with its needle-sharp, venom-coated spines.

I came upon one turtle laying. Her egg chamber was half full. The eggs were exactly like Ping-Pong balls, except that they were lubricated by a clear, shining mucus. While I watched, the tail dipped and the ovipositor pumped out another one. It was the old miracle, all over again—the wonder that something so ancient and leathery could produce something so new and glistening.

No one knows how old *Chelonia mydas,* the green turtle, grows to be, but the informed guess is about a century. My laying turtle had probably been an egg herself back in 1884, a mere 50 years after the *Charles Eaton* had wrecked on its reef.

Another big female, in digging her own nest, had exposed the nest of another. Five hatchlings were scrambling up the steep sides of the bowl, and a sixth was pinned under the female's hind flipper. Lifting the flipper, I rescued the sixth, then collected the others. I tried the old experiment. Setting the hatchlings down behind the beach crest, out of sight of the sea, I faced them in the wrong direction. They turned sharp about-faces, scrambled over the crest, and made unerring beelines for the ocean.

The dash for the sea is the crucial moment in any turtle's career. Every atom of a hatchling's being yells "Go for it!" My six hatchlings went. They ran with alternate strokes of their flippers, not the simultaneous strokes by which the big females row across the sand. The first wavelets of the hatchlings' lives struck and lifted them, one by one, off the sand. For a stroke or two underwater, the flippers worked alternately; then instinct or the ocean whispered that a double stroke is better, and the hatchlings zipped away. They vanished into an old and abiding mystery. Where *Chelonia mydas* goes, what it does, how it lives, no human knows. From the day a hatchling leaves the beach to the time, perhaps 50 years later, it first returns to breed, relatively little is known of any species of sea turtle.

From topside, bird islands in the tropical

NEXT PAGES: Fairy basslets, among the most common fish of the Great Detached Reef, swim through pretzel-like gorgonian coral. Though all fairy basslets start life as females, they can switch sex within a few days of hatching. And when a male disappears from a school, a dominant female changes sex to take his place.

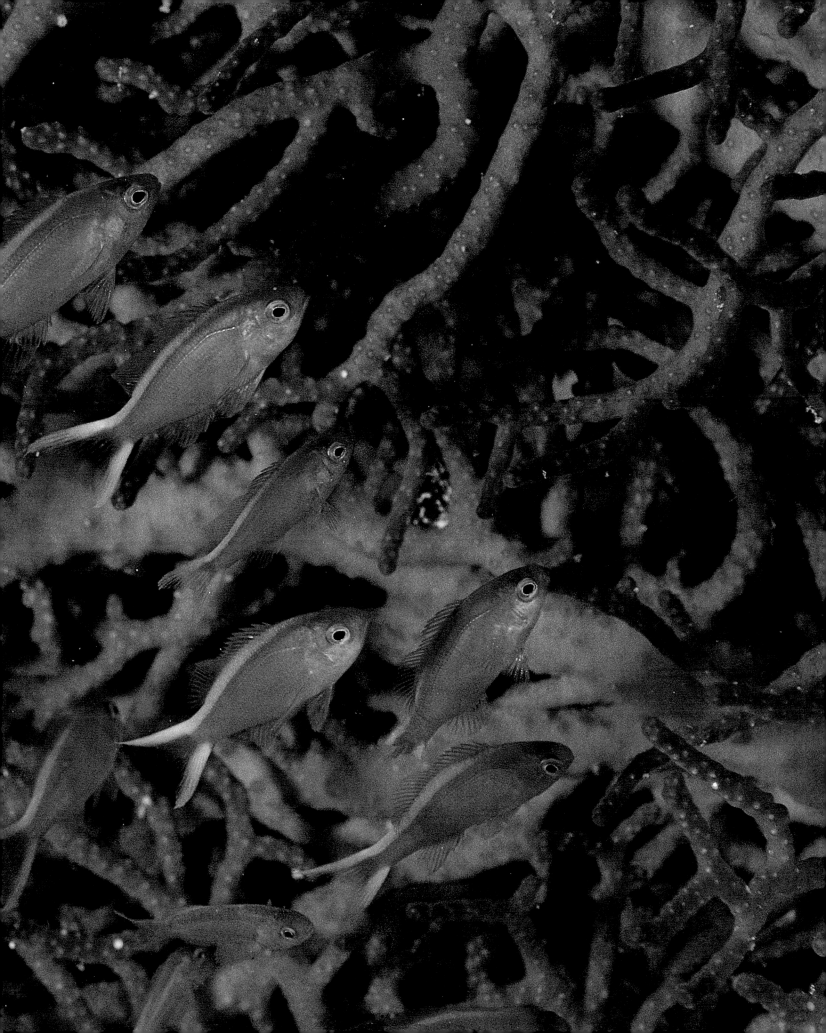

Pacific seem simple places, nothing but sand, turtle tracks, beaks, feathers, guano, and cacophony. That is only the tip of the cay. Small deserts above the surface, coral islets are thriving underneath.

At a depth of 40 feet, the island's leeward slope of sand and coral gardens ended in a sheer, 80-foot cliff of coral rock. Doubilet and I, working our way along the face of the cliff, began encountering turtles resting or asleep in clefts and on ledges. Turtles had stashed themselves at all levels of the cliff face. "A parking lot!" Dave would say afterward. Gravid turtles waiting for nightfall do not simply swim around off the beach, marking time against the current, as I had imagined. Turtles are much more sensible.

We left Raine Island and headed south: Great Detached Reef, Wishbone Reef, Martha Ridgway Reefs, Mantis Reef, Ferguson Reef, nameless reef, Lagoon Reef, nameless reef, nameless reef, nameless reef, nameless reef, Long Sandy Reef, Second

Small Reef, Southern Small Detached Reef, Providential Channel, Log Reef, First Small Reef. I began to sense the endlessness of the Great Barrier. A white line of surf was always breaking on the port side. One morning Rodney Fox, gazing at those far combers that fenced us in, turned from the window and caught my eye. "I've been wondering what it was like in the days of Captain Cook," he said. "No radar. Men going ahead in longboats to take soundings."

Shortly afterward, in the middle of what had seemed an empty blue sea, *Auriga Bay* lost momentum for an instant. I took a half step forward and regained my balance. The engine rose in pitch, then seemed about to stall, and the buzzer of the bilge alarm sounded. At the far end of the same instant, we came free of whatever we had hit, and the ocean returned our momentum to us.

"Whyle," Graham joked, without smiling. "Whyle" is Australian for whale. It was not a cetacean we had hit, however; it was a

Doctor-barber of the deep, a striped cleaner wrasse removes parasites and detritus from a spotted coral trout and helps keep its client disease free. Though the trout could easily swallow the tiny wrasse, it checks its predatory instincts during grooming sessions—an example of symbiosis.

Like hungry dogs, potato cod (above) nip at a diver until he serves the plat du jour: sliced fish fillets. In return, the cod, which weigh up to 150 pounds, let people hug, stroke, or even kiss them.

bommie. Graham checked our position, found we had shaded off course, and spun the helm to starboard.

That was how it had been in the days of Capt. James Cook, I thought. Every captain who sails coral seas dings a bommie now and then, and surely Cook had dinged his share.

Bligh Reef, Bligh Boat Entrance, nameless reef, nameless reef, nameless reef, Cat Reef, Derry Reef, Ham Reef, Franklin Reef. Then Tijou Reef. Tijou is a big reef, 14 miles long. In our first dive on Tijou, at 110 feet deep on a steep sandy slope, we encountered several 6-foot sharks, silvertips, *Carcharhinus albimarginatus*. The silvertip is one species a diver needs to watch out for. Something in the robustness of the sharks, or in the bold way they carried themselves, would have told us so, had we not already known it. The sharks disappeared, and we swam down after them.

There is a spookiness, sharks or not, to the way a seaward ribbon reef like Tijou slopes down to its drop-off. The whiteness of the sand, blue-tinted by depth, angles sharply down toward a blue oblivion. The pressure increases, your wet suit compresses, you gain weight and speed. The blue oblivion is sucking you down. You brake by punching short blasts of air into your buoyancy compensator, but these never seem enough to offset the pull of void. At 160 feet, passing over the edge of the drop-off, our stomachs tried to call us back. We backpaddled. Circling just under the lip were the five silvertips. They came up to look us over, then disappeared over the edge.

When the Great Barrier resumed its demonstration of sand cays, the lesson seemed to run backward. The cays were not evolving toward wooded islands; they were regressing toward the simplicity of their origins. Sand Bank No. 8 was a small cay that had no proper name. We arrived at 5:30 in the afternoon, the hour the birds were thickest. Graham and I went ashore in the

Complete with swimming pool and tennis courts, the world's first floating resort prepares for its grand opening in a sheltered lagoon of the John Brewer Reef, 43 miles from Townsville. Should a storm strike, the 200-room, 11,000-ton hotel will turn on its mooring and point into the wind. Guests will arrive by seaplane, helicopter, or catamaran, like the one at left that takes tourists on day trips from the coast to the outer reefs.

tin boat to walk around.

No. 8 was treeless, with turtle tracks around its margins and a five o'clock shadow of pioneer vegetation covering its interior. The cay was inhabited mostly by sooty terns. In the general sootiness of the dominant colony, an enclave of bridled terns made a gray streak. There were some brown boobies as well, and a few silver gulls hung in small gangs around the beach, waiting to steal unguarded tern eggs. Graham and I were halfway around the island before I saw three crested terns. "Crested terns," I said, amending my list.

Graham grunted, not much interested. "That looks like Gordon's Gin," he announced. He walked over to a bottle half buried in sand. Gordon's Gin it was. "Johnny Walker," he added, of a distant glint of glass. Then, "That's Bundaberg." The captain was right nearly every time. He took a birder's pleasure in his identifications. He smiled fondly down on each sea-glazed bottle, as if at memories of good times shared.

After sundown the white sand of a cay radiates an afterlight, a kind of sea-level alpenglow—a cayglow. From the deck of *Auriga Bay* we watched the cayglow on No. 8. Turtles began hauling out on the beach. They were like dark steamer trunks washed ashore from some wreck, except that now and again one moved. The cayglow died and the sky filled with stars. Terns continued to pass over the boat, crying and bickering in the night sky. Peering up toward the cries, I could see no birds, only the southern constellations. It was as if the stars themselves had taken to conversing in tern language.

We continued south. Sand Bank No. 7, nameless reef, nameless reef, nameless reef, Sand Bank No. 6, nameless reef, Sand Bank No. 5, nameless reef, Rodda Reef, Joan Reef, Wilson Reef, Davie Reef, Tydeman Reef, Snake Reef, Crescent Reef, Fly Reef, Jewell Reef, Hilder Reef, Hicks Reef.

Lizard Island.

A diver peers into a *bommie* (opposite), a submerged chunk of hard coral. Another bommie in the Agincourt Reefs—this one a table coral (above left)—shelters tiny gobies (above). Its flat surface captures maximum sunlight so the algae in its tissues can photosynthesize organic compounds that the coral polyps use as food. Some bommies are 2,000 years old.

After weeks of cruising coral reefs and cays, seascapes of low relief become the rule, and a high continental island comes as a shock. Lizard Island rose mountainous ahead of us, its rocky ridges bathed in an overexposed, Maxfield Parrish sort of light. It looked mythical, like an island from Homer or Virgil. We admired the ridges, the rock outcrops, *the actual trees*. As we coasted the northern shore, Steve Sheehan, the engineer, pointed out the trail to Cook's Look, the island's summit. "Cook finally got tired of mucking around and bumping into things," Steve said, "so he climbed up there to see where he was." That was how it had been. Captain Cook had sailed 600 miles inside the Great Barrier Reef before realizing it was there. He had entered at the southern end, where the continental shelf is widest and the reef farthest from shore. Traveling northward, dutifully charting the Australian coast as the reef pinched in on him, he had suddenly found himself "barrocaded with Shoals." From Cook's Look, Steve said, there was a fine panorama. You could see Cook's Passage, the escape route Cook had spotted from the mountain and through which he had sailed his battered *Endeavour* in 1770. You could also see the Cod Hole, our next destination.

The Cod Hole is a feeding station, a cove on the outer reef where humans have been entertaining potato cod for a decade. The potato cod, *Epinephelus tukula*, is a giant, girthy, mottled, spectacularly homely fish with an enormous downturned mouth. On entering the Cod Hole, we were immediately surrounded by 15 or 16 of them. Graham swam down with a 5-gallon plastic jug filled with cut-up Spanish mackerel. He stationed himself atop a coral head, and the cod abandoned the rest of us to press in close around him. One big cod took position inches in front of Graham's face mask, staring into his eyes. This boldest cod was accompanied by a remora, which in anticipation of food had detached from its host

285

A clown fish (far left) lives in protective harmony among a sea anemone's venomous tentacles. Clown fish build up an immunity to the stinging cells that anemones use to paralyze prey.

A harlequin tusk fish (upper) grazes on the lagoon floor, crushing shells with its sharp blue teeth. Bobbing among coral branches, beaked leatherjackets (above) feed on coral polyps and small crustaceans at the reef's edge. A canary blenny (left) seeks shelter inside a coral crevice, swiveling one eye to scout for danger.

and was swimming excited circles and half-loops underneath. Another cod had a tiny golden trevally for its sidekick. The big fish and the tiny fish circled together, the trevally holding position always in the same spot below the cod's chin. There were territorial skirmishes, big cod waddling after smaller cod to chase them away. "Like blimps," Dave Doubilet would say later. "Like big dogs," his wife, Annie, would say. Blue-banded seaperch swarmed about Graham's legs, sometimes obscuring them. If the cod were the dogs at this feeding, then the perch rubbing his legs were the cats.

Graham began the feeding. A cod turned away with the silvery head of a Spanish mackerel held dead center in its mouth, like a cigar. The cod inhaled and the head vanished. Graham's glove and feeding hand disappeared into the mouth of a big cod. For a moment the cod would not give the hand back. When the hand did come free, Graham playfully punched the fish with it, a reprimand. Another rude fish stole a chunk of fish over Graham's shoulder, and he gave that fish the finger. Cod and coincidence were so thick about him that his gesture happened to travel up the cloaca of an innocent cod passing overhead—much to that cod's surprise and Graham's own.

Yonge Reef, No Name Reef, Ribbon Reef No. 10, Ribbon Reef No 9., Ribbon Reef No. 8, No. 7, No. 6, 5, 4, 3, 2, 1, Endeavour Reef, Cape Tribulation.

From Port Douglas, below Cape Tribulation, in the middle of the Cairns Section of the park, we caught a ride on one of the big catamarans of Quicksilver Cruises out to a pontoon the company keeps moored on one of the Agincourt Reefs. There we witnessed an animal aggregation as startling, in its way, as any on the Great Barrier Reef. We went overboard with platoons of novice snorkelers. Of the great spectacles on the reef—writhing convocations of spawning sea snakes, opalescent armies of parrotfish on their breeding marches—few can be as

Sooty terns swoop down to a sand cay north of Lizard Island. On the ground, when plant material is scarce, brown boobies lay eggs in nests fashioned of shells, feathers, corals—even dead sea snakes. A young booby (above) surveys the cay, a low island built of coral debris and sand swept into formation by the waves.

Every summer on Barrier Reef islands, thousands of green turtles emerge from the sea to perform an age-old ritual. In the dark a female lays about a hundred leathery eggs inside an egg chamber (above left) on the beach. At dawn she flips sand backward to conceal her nest full of eggs (opposite); the temperature of the sand will determine the sex of the hatchlings. Tears (above) protect her eyes from sand and also excrete salt absorbed from seawater.

dumbfounding as the furious dance of humans learning to snorkel.

A balding German in his mid-30s pedaled desperately on his fins, like a man riding a unicycle. His wife or girlfriend, sculling calmly beside him, tried to tell him to relax. He nodded but continued racing his unicycle. A hairy-chested man held his arms ahead of him, bringing his fingers to a point to form a cutwater. The prow of his arms passed me, then the dark fur rug of his chest and abdomen, finally the bubbly screws of his fins. A great, beamy Australian matron churned by, a dreadnought. A boy, not five seconds in the water, pointed frantically beneath him. *"Mmmmmmm!"* he piped through his snorkel. *"Mmmmmmhhh! Mmmmeeeeeeuuuuummhh!"* To hear him, one would have thought that a school of hammerheads had just turned toward him. In fact, it was just reef rapture. He had taken his first underwater look at the polychrome reality of the reef.

At the bottom of the Great Barrier Reef, 970 miles south of Raine Island, the reef concluded our lessons on sand cays. Heron Island, in the park's Capricornia Section, is a wooded cay of a classic sort. The interior of the island is a stand of *Pisonia grandis,* the

monarch of sandy forest all across the tropical Pacific. Heron Island is the Great Barrier Reef Marine Park in microcosm. The island is a resort, a research station, a bird colony, a wildlife sanctuary—everything a national marine park should be.

One hundred thousand white-capped noddy terns nest on Heron. Every pisonia tree on the island is noisy with dozens of them. There is no need for rakes on Heron. A fallen leaf scarcely hits the ground before it is borne aloft again in the beak of a tern, stolen by a second tern, and added to a nest. Flying noddies narrowly miss you as you walk the sand avenues between the bungalows of the resort. Standing noddies scarcely bother to step aside for you. A plume or two of noddy down is always wafting around the bathroom of your bungalow, and noddy bombers score three or four direct hits daily on your hat and shoulders. Yet life among the birds is surprisingly agreeable.

Forty thousand wedge-tailed shearwaters spend each night in sand burrows on the island. Australians call shearwaters "muttonbirds"—they are said to be good to eat—but a commoner common name is "moaning bird." The moaning begins shortly after dusk, a semihuman caterwauling. The first

A green turtle lumbers back to the sea (opposite), leaving behind a distinctive trail—and a new generation. About eight weeks later a hatchling hits the water with a flying swim stroke, perhaps to face a carnivorous fish. Some babies never even reach the ocean; this one dodged silver gulls and ghost crabs hunting on the beach.

night on Heron Island is like being a passenger on the ship that carries zombie children to hell. By the second night, the moaning has become a lullaby, and you have trouble sleeping without it.

We seldom strayed far afield in our dives on Heron Island. Most of our time underwater was spent on a bommie just outside the channel to the pier. It was a rich spot, and we returned again and again. There were batfish on the Heron bommie, vampire triggerfish, moray eels, Spanish dancers, tusk fish of several species, a wide selection of wrasses. We found a wobbegong shark there one day, a sorry-looking, camouflaged creature, its mouth frilled outlandishly to break up the telltale line of the jaws.

The coral reef is commonly thought to be an undersea jungle, a place of savage and relentless Darwinian struggle. The big fish swallows the smaller fish swallows the smaller fish, as in cartoons. In fact, even the jungle is not such a jungle. In complex ecosystems like the tropical rain forest and the tropical reef, what strikes the observer is not the competition but the cooperation.

We seldom saw predation on the Great Barrier Reef. Sharks cruised by us on nearly every dive, but we never saw a shark eat anything. The tentacles of anemones were always stirring in the current, but we never saw one latch onto anything. Once I saw a small goby in the mouth of a wrasse. That was about all the violence we witnessed. What we did see daily, and everywhere, was symbiosis. The art most intricately elaborated on the reef—perhaps more highly developed there than in any other ecosystem—is the art of living together.

The symbiotic relationship between coral polyps and zooxanthellae, the tiny one-celled plants they harbor in their tissues, is the foundation of the reef. Zooxanthellae distinguish reef-building corals from the inconspicuous coral colonies of colder waters. The reef is the tropical coral's means of keeping its zooxanthellae in sunlight, so

293

they can photosynthesize and produce food for both plant and polyp. The bedrock of the reef is not so much coral limestone as it is mutual need.

The cleaner wrasse is the most conspicuous symbiont on the reef. It is *everybody's* symbiont, ready and willing to remove dead skin or parasites from fish or man or reptile. At cleaner stations fish line up, waiting their turn, a coral trout behind a sweetlip emperor behind a blue tusk fish. The parasite removal service is vital; in areas where the cleaner fish have been experimentally removed, most fish quickly depart for another cleaning station.

A cleaner wrasse signals its readiness to clean by doing a strange, eye-catching dance. Its rear end lifts exuberantly again and again, but the head stays in place; the wrasse bounces like a hot rod revving at an intersection. A slingjaw wrasse signals its readiness to be cleaned by holding itself at a steep angle and extending its remarkably protrusible mouth parts. Small, schooling species are often skittish at cleaning stations. The banana fish hold themselves vertically, signaling readiness, but are giggly and ticklish when the cleaner approaches.

We spent hours watching the odd symbiosis between blind shrimp and the small gobies. The arrangement was triangular: two shrimp and one goby. The goby stood watch at the entrance to the hole while the shrimp maintained it, pushing sand out like tiny

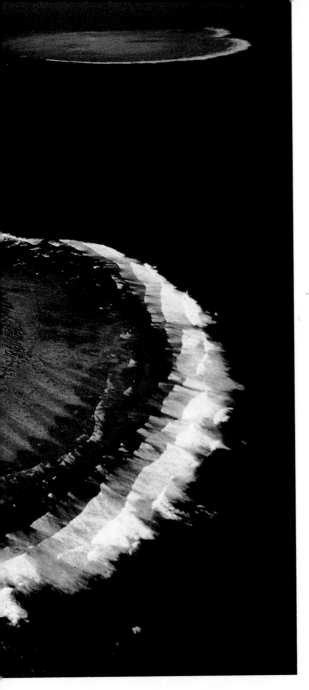

Coral reefs surround Wreck Island, named after a grounded whaleboat; zoning allows limited scientific research here. Nearby Heron Island, its namesake the resident reef heron (right), plays host to tourists as well as birds. A buff-banded rail (above right), common on South Pacific islands, protects its chick.

tractors. Satisfied that the hole was in order, the shrimp would dig trenches away from the entrance, mining the sand for small edible things. Now and again the goby would dart forward to nip off something the shrimp had stirred up. When danger threatened, the goby darted for the hole, and all three vanished in a single puff of sand.

Strange bedfellows! Watching them together, I had nothing but questions. How did such a relationship ever evolve? How had this particular pair of blind shrimp found their goby? How do they introduce themselves? What are the sleeping arrangements in the burrow?

Whenever one of the shrimp, bulldozing, advanced beyond where the goby had stationed itself, the crustacean laid one long antenna back over the fish, reassuring itself that the coast was clear. That antenna, resting nearly invisible on the goby's back, was a nice symbol, I thought.

The Great Barrier Reef is an edifice of connections. Working in concert, through webs of mutual dependencies infinitely complex, the reef's corals, cementing algae, tube worms, fish, echinoderms, bivalves, crustaceans, and sponges have a collective intelligence. Together they do architecture. Among other clever engineering projects, they somehow conspire to build the tongue-and-groove system of the reef front. From the seaward side of the reef, tongues of coral extend outward against the march of the swells. The tongues deflect incoming waves into the grooves between, where the ocean expends its energy against itself, arriving at the reef much mollified.

Coral reefs are more than places. They are a kind of superorganism. In the genus of coral reefs, the Great Barrier is the largest specimen, a great, growing, many-souled, serpentine creature, its tail wrapped about the Tropic of Capricorn, its head more than halfway to the Equator.

By Kenneth Brower
Photographs by David Doubilet

Swimming precariously close to danger, a diver need not fear a black-spotted ray unless he disturbs this 340-pound creature, capable of whipping its tail and planting a venomous barb in an intruder's body. Man and beast coexist for now in this fragile ecosystem, but the Great Barrier Reef's survival depends on the wise stewardship of humans.

Astrakhan' State Nature Reserve
Director
Naberezhnaya reka Tsarev 119
Astrakhan'
U.S.S.R. 414021

Banff National Park
Superintendent
Box 900
Banff, Alberta
Canada T0L 0C0

Chobe National Park and
Moremi Wildlife Reserve
Tourism Division
Private Bag 0047
Gaborone, Botswana

Fiordland National Park
Park Headquarters
P.O. Box 29
Te Anau, New Zealand

Great Barrier Reef Marine Park
Authority
Chairman
P.O. Box 1379
Townsville, Queensland 4810
Australia

Great Basin National Park
Superintendent
Baker, Nevada 89311

Jasper National Park
Superintendent
P.O. Box 10
Jasper, Alberta
Canada T0E 1E0

Kavkaz State Nature Reserve
Director
Street Karl Marx 8
Sochi-341-Adler
U.S.S.R. 354341

Kootenay National Park
Superintendent
Radium Hot Springs
British Columbia
Canada V0A 1M0

Lake District National Park
Park Management and Visitor
Services
National Park Office
Brockhole
Windermere
Cumbria LA 23 1LJ
England

Manú Biosphere Reserve
Administrador
Heladeros 157
Of. 34 Apartado 1057
Cuzco, Peru

Prioksko-Terrasnyy State Nature
Reserve
Director
P.O. Danki
Moscow Region
U.S.S.R. 142274

Ranthambhore National Park
Field Director
Sawai Madhopur
Rajasthan, India

Yellowstone National Park
Superintendent
P.O. Box 168
Yellowstone National Park,
Wyoming 82190

Yoho National Park
Superintendent
Box 99
Field, British Columbia
Canada V0A 1G0

We are grateful to the many individuals, groups, and institutions who helped in the preparation of *Nature's Wonderlands: National Parks of the World.* Our special thanks go to Jeremy Harrison of the International Union for Conservation of Nature and Natural Resources and Ronald W. Cooksy, Robert C. Milne, and John Poppeliers, all with the National Park Service.

For the chapter on Yellowstone and Great Basin National Parks, we wish to thank Al Hendricks, Thomas McNamee, Michael Mantell, Roderick Nash, Steve Oulman, Sandra Robinson, Paul Schullery.

For the Canadian Rockies, Bill Browne, Perry Jacobson, Rick Kunelius, Ivor Petrak, Dan Strickland, Jon Whyte, John G. Woods.

For the national parks and reserves in Botswana, Alec Campbell, Karen Ross Greer, Diana McMeekin, Eleanor Warr, Kalahari Conservation Society.

For the Lake District National Park, Paul Betz and Ronald Sands.

For the reserves in the Soviet Union, Carolyn McMartin, Mary Meade Nash, Philip R. Pryde, Alexei Pushkov, Nikolai Romanov, Shelley L. Sperry, Vadim Tetevin.

For Manú Biosphere Reserve, Terry Erwin, Robin Foster, Kim Hill, Charles Munn, Ken Petren, John Terborgh.

For Ranthambhore National Park, Jaswant Singh Nathawat.

For Fiordland National Park, D.G. Bishop and Ron Peacock.

For the Great Barrier Reef Marine Park, Frederick Bayer, Deborah Bell, Graeme G. Kelleher, Colin J. Limpus, R.J. McKay, Victor Springer, George Zug.

For the continental essays, we would like to thank the following individuals: Robert Birkholz-Lambrecht, Catarina Bjurholm, Mimi Brian, Broughton Coburn, Edward Cresto, Holly Dublin, Jon W. Erickson, Richard Estes, John G. Galaty, William J. Hamilton III, John Marsh, L. David Mech, Raymundo Punongbayan, Kelvin Rodolfo, Mary K. Seely, R.L. Singh, Franco Tassi, K. Thiele, Birgir Thorgilsson, Rick Weyerhaeuser.

We are also indebted to the National Geographic Administrative Services, Library/News Collection, Messenger Service, Pre-Press/Typographic, Translation Division, and Travel Office.

The staff consulted many references in the preparation of this volume. Three helpful books of a general nature are *National Parks, Conservation and Development: The Role of Protected Areas in Sustaining Society* edited by Jeffrey A. McNeely and Kenton R. Miller; *Our World's Heritage* published by the National Geographic Society; and *Biodiversity* edited by Edward O. Wilson.

The reader may wish to consult the references cited below.

For the chapter on Yellowstone and Great Basin National Parks: *A Sand County Almanac* by Aldo Leopold; *The Grizzly Bear* by Thomas McNamee; *Wilderness and the American Mind* by Roderick Nash; *National Parks: The American Experience* by Alfred Runte; *Mountain Time* by Paul Schullery.

For the Canadian Rockies: *The Canadian Rockies: Early Travels and Explorations* by Esther Fraser; *Handbook of the Canadian Rockies* by Ben Gadd; *Mountain Sheep: A Study in Behavior and Evolution* by Valerius Geist; *Men for the Mountains* by Sid Marty.

For the national parks and reserves in Botswana: *The Lions and Elephants of the Chobe* by Bruce Aiken; *Botswana: A Brush with the Wild* by Paul Augustinus; *The Guide to Botswana* by Alec Campbell; *Okavango, Jewel of the Kalahari* by Karen Ross.

For the Lake District National Park: *Land of the Lakes* by Melvyn Bragg; *A Walk Around the Lakes* by Hunter Davies; *Cumbrian Discovery* by Molly Lefebure; *Cumbria* by John Parker; *Life and Tradition in the Lake District* by William Rollinson.

For the reserves in the Soviet Union: *The Natural History of the U.S.S.R.* by Algirdas Knystautas; *Conservation in the Soviet Union* by Philip R. Pryde; *Models of Nature* by Douglas R. Weiner.

For Manú Biosphere Reserve: *In the Rainforest* by Catherine Caufield and *The Primary Source* by Norman Myers.

For Ranthambhore National Park: *Saving the Tiger* by Guy Mountfort; *With Tigers in the Wild* by Fateh Singh Rathore, Tejbir Singh, and Valmik Thapar; *The Deer and the Tiger* by George B. Schaller; *Tiger! Tiger!* by Arjan Singh; *Tiger: Portrait of a Predator* by Valmik Thapar.

For Fiordland National Park: *Greenstone Trails: The Maori Search for Pounamu* by Barry Brailsford; *Immigrant Killers* by Carolyn King; *Mountains of Water: The Story of Fiordland National Park* by the New Zealand Department of Lands and Survey.

For the Great Barrier Reef Marine Park: *The Great Barrier Reef* by Isobel Bennett; *So Excellent A Fishe* by Archie Carr; *Australia's Great Barrier Reef* by Robert Endean; *Reader's Digest Book of the Great Barrier Reef*.

JENNIFER GORHAM ACKERMAN, an editor and writer in National Geographic Book Service, specializes in science and natural history. Her work has appeared in National Geographic books and other publications.

JAMES BALOG's photographs can be seen in *Smithsonian*, NATIONAL GEOGRAPHIC, and *A Day in the Life of the Soviet Union*. His newest book is *Survivors of Eden*, studio portraits of endangered wildlife species. He lives in Boulder, Colorado.

IAN BERRY is a photographer whose work has appeared in *Geo, Paris Match,* and *Life*. He has contributed to numerous books, and has exhibited his work in France and in his native England.

JIM BRANDENBURG joined the National Geographic Society as a contract photographer in 1978. For his book and television special *White Wolf: Living with an Arctic Legend*, he spent months camped next to a wolf den.

KENNETH BROWER's interest in Pacific cultures and ecology has taken him to Alaska, Borneo, Micronesia, and Australia. He is the author of numerous books, including *The Starship and the Canoe*. He lives in Oakland, California.

DOUGLAS H. CHADWICK, a frequent contributor to National Geographic publications, lives in Whitefish, Montana, at the edge of Glacier National Park. His assignments have taken him to Nepal, Africa, the Amazon, and the Soviet Union.

BILL CURTSINGER is a National Geographic contract photographer who has traveled from the Seychelles to beneath Antarctic ice. His photographs also illustrate *The Pine Barrens* and *Wake of the Whale*. He lives in Maine.

DAVID DOUBILET began diving at age 8 and took his first underwater photographs at 12. Since 1972, when his photographs first appeared in NATIONAL GEOGRAPHIC, he has illustrated more than 25 articles. He lives in New York City with his wife, Anne, and their daughter, Emily.

FRANS LANTING is an economist-turned-photographer specializing in natural history. His photographs have appeared in many popular and scientific publications and he is a co-author of several books. When not traveling, he lives in Santa Cruz, California.

GEORGE F. MOBLEY joined the photography staff of the National Geographic Society 27 years ago. He has produced work from every continent, and he has been to India several times. He lives on a small farm in Virginia's Shenandoah Valley.

ROBERT M. POOLE, an assistant editor for NATIONAL GEOGRAPHIC, has traveled to China, Sweden, England, and Oceania on assignments. He has also written for the *New York Times*, the *Washington Post*, and the *Boston Globe*.

NORMAN SHRAPNEL is an award-winning columnist for the *Guardian*. He lives in Gloucester, England.

PAUL THEROUX, author of best-selling travel books such as *The Great Railway Bazaar* and *Riding the Iron Rooster*, has also published numerous novels. He is an American who divides his time between Cape Cod and London.

JONATHAN B. TOURTELLOT, an editor and writer in National Geographic Book Service, has visited Africa three times, writing about parks in Tanzania, Kenya, Rwanda, Zaïre, and Botswana.

JERE VAN DYK is a free-lance writer living in New York. His book, *In Afghanistan*, recounts how he sneaked into that country to live with guerillas opposing Soviet troops in 1981. He has also written for NATIONAL GEOGRAPHIC.

GEOFFREY C. WARD is a former editor of *Audience* and *American Heritage* magazines. He spent several boyhood years in India and writes often about that country and its wildlife. He lives in New York City.

ART WOLFE is a free-lancer who specializes in wildlife photography. His work has appeared in many publications and books. Currently his projects include books about the Alaskan wilderness and North American owls. His home is in Seattle.

Type composition by the Typographic section
of National Geographic Production Services,
Pre-Press Division. Color separations by
Chanticleer Co., Inc., New York, N.Y.; The
Lanman Companies, Washington, D. C.;
Lincoln Graphics Inc., Cherry Hill, N.J.
Printed and bound by R. R. Donnelly & Sons
Co., Chicago, Ill. Paper by Mead Paper Co.,
New York, N.Y.

Library of Congress ᴄɪᴘ Data

Nature's wonderlands: national parks of the
world.

        p.   cm.
    Bibliography: p.
    Includes index.
        ISBN 0-87044-766-1 (alk. paper).—ISBN
    0-87044-768-8 (1 lib. bdg.: alk. paper).—
    ISBN 0-87044-767-X (deluxe: alk. paper)
        1. National parks and reserves
    I. National Geographic Society (U. S.)
    SB481.N37 1989
    363.6'8—dc20   89-3292
                                          CIP